A Theology of Mission for Myanmar

Christian Mission in the Context
of Buddhist Nat Worship

J. Pau D. Lian

ACADEMIC

© 2025 J. Pau D. Lian

Published 2025 by Langham Academic
An imprint of Langham Publishing
www.langhampublishing.org

Langham Publishing and its imprints are a ministry of Langham Partnership

Langham Partnership
PO Box 296, Carlisle, Cumbria, CA3 9WZ, UK
www.langham.org

ISBNs:
978-1-78641-120-4 Print
978-1-78641-301-7 ePub
978-1-78641-302-4 PDF
DOI: https://doi.org/10.69811/9781786411204

J. Pau D. Lian has asserted his right under the Copyright, Designs and Patents Act, 1988 to be identified as the Author of this work.

All rights reserved. No part of this publication may be reproduced, stored in a retrieval system or transmitted, in any form or by any means, electronic, mechanical, photocopying, recording or otherwise, without the prior written permission of the publisher or the Copyright Licensing Agency.

Requests to reuse content from Langham Publishing are processed through PLSclear. Please visit www.plsclear.com to complete your request.

All Scripture quotations, unless otherwise indicated, are taken from The Holy Bible, English Standard Version® (ESV®), copyright © 2001 by Crossway, a publishing ministry of Good News Publishers. Used by permission. All rights reserved.

Scripture quotations marked (NIV) are taken from the Holy Bible, New International Version®, NIV®. Copyright © 1973, 1978, 1984, 2011 by Biblica, Inc.™ Used by permission of Zondervan.

Scripture quotations marked (NKJV) are taken from the New King James Version. Copyright © 1982 by Thomas Nelson, Inc. Used by permission. All rights reserved.

British Library Cataloguing-in-Publication Data
A catalogue record for this book is available from the British Library

ISBN: 978-1-78641-120-4

Cover & Book Design: projectluz.com

Langham Partnership actively supports theological dialogue and an author's right to publish but does not necessarily endorse the views and opinions set forth here or in works referenced within this publication, nor can we guarantee technical and grammatical correctness. Langham Partnership does not accept any responsibility or liability to persons or property as a consequence of the reading, use or interpretation of its published content.

To my dad, Ngul Za Go and my Mum, Dim Za Ning, and to my wife, Nang Nyo Me San and son, Go Mun Tuang
"If any of you lacks wisdom, let him ask God, who gives generously to all without reproach, and it will be given him."
James 1:5

Contents

Acknowledgments ix

Abbreviations xi

Chronology xiii

Glossary xv

Abstract xix

Chapter 1 1
Introduction, Missiological Problem, and Rationale
    Introduction 1
    Assumption and Presupposition 6
    Research Concern 10
    Missiological Rationale 12
    The Research Problem 18
    Limitation and Delimitation 21
    Research Questions 23
    Preliminary Research Approach/Method 25

Chapter 2 29
Scriptural and Confessional Considerations and Literature Review
    Burmese Worldview 29
        God in Myanmar 33
        Problem of Natural Evil in Burmese Context 34
        Missionaries and Contemporary Theologians' Attitudes
            Toward Nat Worship 37
    Missiological Reflections on Christ, Church, and Nat Worship 42
        The Suffering of Christ in Response to Nat Worship 48
        Gospel through Suffering 53
        The Suffering Church 58
    The Role of Nat Worship Informs Life in Society 65
        Life after Death 67
        Religious Ceremony 69
        Sacred and Profane in Nat Worship 71

Chapter 3 75
Research Approach, Design, and Procedures
    Interview Findings 78

Research Approach 79
Research Design 80
Research Procedures 82

Chapter 4 85
Research Findings and Analysis
Interview Responses 87
Online Responses for Nat Worship and Christianity 95

Chapter 5 117
Research Summary, Conclusions, Implications, and Recommendations
Conclusions 118
Implications 120
Recommendations for Further Research 123

Bibliography 127

Scripture Index 137

Acknowledgments

First and foremost, I want to thank the Almighty God for the unfailing grace and love for granting me good health in body, mind, and spirit to carry me through the journey of this academic research. I also would like to register my gratitude to Concordia Theological Seminary, Fort Wayne, for accepting me and the financial assistance that enabled me to continue my PhD studies. Second, I would like to express my profound gratitude to the Langham International Scholarship for funding my PhD studies. Third, for this academic work, I am deeply indebted to my advisor Dr. Walter A. Maier III who tirelessly checked my manuscript and encouraged me to undertake this project. He deserves my special thanks for his guidance and support.

I would like to acknowledge my heartfelt gratitude to Dr. Klaus Detlev Schulz, the director of Doctor of Philosophy in Missiology, who gave me new insights and shaped my thoughts; without his directions, this work would not achieve this level. Dr. Matthew Buse has been a fixer when formatting problems occurred; I am fortunate to have his talents in working with technology. Dr. Joshua Pagan's analytical mind helped me to design my research questions. Without the assistance and support of the Emmanuel Christian Church, Indianapolis, I would not have been able to complete my research. My acknowledgments cannot be concluded without mentioning my dear and loving wife, Nang Nyo Me San and our dear son, Go Mun Tuang for the patience, love, and support I have received from them. They always prayed for my studies and provided warmth and comfort I most needed, especially in times when I became frustrated with the research work.

Abbreviations

ABM	American Baptist Missionary
ESV	English Standard Version
IMC	International Missionary Council
MBC	Myanmar Baptist Convention
MIT	Myanmar Institute of Theology
NIV	New International Version
TBCY	Tedim Baptist Church-Yangon
WCC	World Council of Churches

Chronology

The arrival of Buddhism   300 B.C.
The arrival of Roman Catholicism   A.D. 1740
The arrival of Protestant Christianity   A.D. 1813

Glossary

Buddhism:	religion founded by Gautama, the Buddha
Bta:	religion
Burmese:	the people and language of Burma
Lumyo:	national
Min Mahagiri:	kings of bad angels
Mithun:	a domestic animal in Myanmar
Nat:	god-like spirits venerated in Myanmar
Nat kadaw:	a spirit medium
Nat pwe:	ambivalent spirit
Paritta:	sutra uttered by the Buddha to protect devotees
Pali:	a middle Indo-Aryan liturgical language
Shinbyu:	novitiation or ordination in Buddhism
Thavara:	eternal
Thakhin:	lord, master, Lord
Thakyamin:	kings of good angels
Phaya or hpaya:	god or God
Zayat:	a small tent or shelter erected normally beside the road in Myanmar

Abstract

This dissertation aims to respond to the contemporary Myanmar theologians' attempt to reconcile Nat worship with Christianity, necessitating a renewed call for a Christian mission in Myanmar. Two hundred years after the first missionary arrived in the country, some evangelical Christians noticed the stagnant Christian faith and the influence of Buddhist-Nat worship. A mixture of Buddhism and Nat worship practice has been a significant part of Myanmar's tradition and customs. This study shows that Nat worship is still practiced differently and has influenced Christianity in Myanmar. The prevalence of Nat worship is evident as only 6.2 percent of Myanmar's population claims to be Christian.

This dissertation argues that a theology of mission must be grounded on a Trinitarian *missio Dei* and the Scripture with specific focus on *missio Christi* and *ecclesiae*. A theology of mission anchored to soteriology and ecclesiology is the inseparable connection between the message of salvation, the nature of the church, and the mission of God. Through the historical library research, the researcher concludes that the mission of God rooted in a Trinitarian framework is critical to responding to syncretistic Christians in Myanmar. Most notably, the dissertation attempts to determine whether or not elements of Nat worship can be congruent with a theology of Christian mission, as liberal Christians think all religions lead to the same truth. Despite a syncretistic Christian influence, the researcher proves that Buddhist-Nat worship contains fundamentally a form of idolatry contrary to the teaching of the Bible and therefore does not cohere with the *missio Dei*. The research's fundamental premise is the ultimate authority of a Trinitarian *missio Dei* rooted in the word of God.

In this qualitative study, invaluable historical data is gained through library research and structured interviews to identify the elements that might support the mission of God in the context of Nat worship. To achieve this purpose, the researcher conducted historical research and interviewed thirteen participants among Myanmar people. In addition, a literature review focuses on scholarly sources on the relationship between the Christian faith and Burmese Nat worship. The literature review and structured interview reveal different relationships between Burmese Nat worship and Christianity for centuries. Through historical library research, the researcher concludes that the mission of God rooted in a Trinitarian framework is key in responding to syncretistic Christians in Myanmar.

CHAPTER 1

Introduction, Missiological Problem, and Rationale

Introduction

The primary purpose of this research is to respond to the contemporary Myanmar liberal Christians by making a solid case for a theology of mission grounded on a Trinitarian *missio Dei*. Second, this study explores, as a result of Christian syncretism with Nat[1] worship, why Myanmar Christians are stagnant in their faith even after celebrating the bicentennial ceremony of Christian arrival. Third, the researcher outlines the ways for a proper starting point for a theology of mission according to the Scripture that is based on a Trinitarian *missio Dei*.

The liberal Christians rejected the use of the terms "mission and conversion" and endorsed interreligious dialogues and mutual understanding between Christianity and Buddhism in Myanmar. The term mission plays a significant role in conversion as Martin Kahler states "mission is the mother of theology."[2] This study also will show forth the impact of the World Council of Churches (WCC) on the contemporary Myanmar Christians and theologians. This is obvious in the perspective of Myanmar liberal Christians who think it unnecessary to identify with the church as long as one is a Christian.

---

1. Nat are traditional spirits that are the objects of worship in Myanmar. They are spirit beings.
2. Robert, *Christian Mission*, 11.

The bottom line from this perspective is that Christianity and the church had different ends.

The time has come to focus a proper theology of mission which will address the present reality by taking seriously the Trinitarian *missio Dei* for the transformation of liberal Christian churches. Finally, by critically analyzing the research findings from the interviews, the history of Myanmar Christian mission, and the Scripture, the mission of God will be redefined and applied. The goal is that Christian mission in Myanmar will be re-rooted in the Trinitarian *missio Dei* for the building of the kingdom of God. The author of this dissertation has drawn a theology of mission from the concept of a Trinitarian *missio Dei* with a Christocentric and ecclesio-centric focus that is deeply anchored to the Scripture.

The existing theology of mission in Myanmar churches attempts to reconcile Burmese Nat worship with Christian mission. However, the researcher insists that Myanmar churches need to reconcile only with Jesus Christ because the mission of God has one intention, to save mankind. The second person of the Trinity, Jesus Christ, is the only Savior and Mediator which is proclaimed through the church.[3]

To provide a better knowledge of the sociocultural and religiopolitical setting, it is essential to highlight a bird's eye view of the country. The mountainous regions of the country are inhabited by minority ethnic groups such as Chin, Kachin, Kayah, Kayin, Rakhine, and Shan whose pre-Christian religion was a primal religion called Nat worship. The plain area is occupied by the majority ethnic group, Burmans, whose pre-Buddhism religion was a primal religion called Nat worship. One thing is clear from the outset that, to become Christians for the Burmese means they must penetrate two religious layers, Nat worship and Buddhism, while the minor ethnicities have to come directly from the primal religion.

The Myanmar Baptist Convention (MBC) celebrated the 200th anniversary on 13 July 2013, to mark the arrival of Adoniram Judson on 13 July 1813, the first American foreign missionary to Myanmar.[4] However, Christianity has

---

3. Stott, *Basic Christianity*, 30.

4. Park, *Mission History of Asian Churches*, 92. The current researcher was privileged to participate as one of the panelists in the Bicentennial Celebration of Adoniram Judson on 13 July 2013, at Andover Newton Theological School in Boston.

never been a mass movement nor so widespread that it caught the attention of the majority of people in Myanmar. The masses are still in the grip of the conventional religion, Burmese Nat worship, and follow traditional customs and practices. Dutch missionaries in Indonesia encountered a similar situation to Myanmar when their converts returned to traditional ritual practices.[5]

The emergence of Burmese Nat worship with the sociocultural and religiopolitical ideology impedes the penetration of the gospel. Therefore, the missionary Adoniram Judson once said, "It was easier to extract a tooth from the tiger's mouth than to convert a Burmese Buddhist to Christian faith."[6] To respond to Burmese Nat worship with the gospel, Judson introduced the Christian God with the name in Burmese, "*thavara phaya*" (eternal God)[7] and the *zayat* (tent).[8] Why and how Judson used the term, "*thavara phaya*" and *zayat* will be investigated later when considering the *missio Christi* and *missio ecclesiae*.[9] We will explain his choice of names for the Christian God from his study of the Burmese culture and language, Pali.[10] We will also explain his choice of names from his translation of the whole Bible.

The researcher investigated the missiological reasons why the Western missionaries before the arrival of Adoniram Judson were not successful in their mission work. The result was not surprising. The Western missionaries, including Vincentius Sangermano, Richard Marden, James Charter, and Felix Carey were not solely committed to the Great Commission of Jesus Christ. For example, the Burmese king, Bagyidaw, ordered Felix Carey to live at Ava and join the business of the Burmese king so Felix resigned from his missionary work.[11]

Vincentius Sangermano pointed out, "the Burmese did not consider the Christians as a serious threat to Buddhism, and, at best they were enjoying only a modest success."[12] The social service opportunities offered by the

---

5. Keane, *Christian Moderns*, 3.
6. Nyunt, *Mission amidst Pagodas*, xv.
7. Bailey, *Adoniram Judson*, 61.
8. Mathieson, *Judson of Burma*, 89.
9. Walker, "Building a Christian Zayat," 14.
10. Pali is considered to be the original language of Buddhism as Hebrew and Greek are for Christianity.
11. Trager, *Burma through Alien Eyes*, 21.
12. Trager, *Burma through Alien Eyes*, 17.

king had weakened the zeal they had for the mission of God. Because of the social services, Sangermano's reputation continued to grow even after he left Myanmar following the establishment of St. Paul School in Yangon, which is still standing today. However, no record of Burmese conversion to Christian faith was found.

Conversely, Adoniram Judson wasted no time in working on the Bible translation, Burmese dictionary, and preaching the gospel. On the one hand, the Roman Catholic missionaries were not considered a great threat to the Burmese people because they had never attempted to convert the Burmese people. On the other, Judson was shut up in one of the worst prisons in the world for seventeen months as the result of proclaiming that there is only one eternal God, *thavara phaya*, among the Burmese Nat worshipers.[13] In large part due to his influence, Myanmar has the third largest number of Baptists worldwide, after the United States and India.

Two hundred and nine years after the arrival of the Judsons, Myanmar Christians had distorted its Christocentric and ecclesio-centric focus because of the pressures brought about by the Burmese Buddhism and Nat ritual practices. This resulted in a merger of the two. This goes against two fundamental beliefs, however: the desire of God to save all and the necessity of the church for salvation that is through Christ alone.

Karl Rahner was the chief architect of breaking this new ground in 1961. According to Synder, "he encouraged his readers not to underestimate God's love and grace and to think optimistically about the possibilities of salvation outside Christianity."[14] This can be seen also in John Hick's observation. According to Hick, all religions lead to the same destination.[15] It reflects the assertion of a Myanmar theologian, Simon Pau Khan En, "Every religion already had a certain type of revelation which qualifies that religion to be able to relate to God."[16]

For liberal Christians in Myanmar, a reconciliation with Burmese Nat worship endorses and promotes the mission of God. Simon Pau Khan En believes, therefore, that the Burmese traditional religion can no longer be

---

13. Judson, *Life of Adoniram Judson*, 221.
14. Snyder, *Global Good News*, 44.
15. Hick, "Religious Pluralism," 293.
16. En, *Nat Worship*, 265.

condemned as being a heathen or pagan religion. This means that to them, all religions are valid and need not turn to Christianity. In other words, the mediation of Christ and the church becomes unnecessary for the mission of God because the whole world and all its religions have become recipients of God's witness.[17]

The belief that the traditional concept of conversion is no longer required for one to identify with Christianity and the church stands in contrast to the traditional concepts of mission. For example, the missiologist Leslie Newbigin expresses a valid concern, "We have corrupted the word Church by constantly using it in a non-missionary sense."[18] Similarly, he observes the mission of God is incomplete without a clear understanding of who Jesus is.[19] The mission of God is fulfilled in Christ and his church; that is the underpinning of this dissertation.

This dichotomy between the mission of God and sending his Son into the world is the rationale for pursuing this study in Myanmar. In other words, the universalistic option of Myanmar mainstream Christians and theologians who compromise the traditional understanding of Christianity is the underlying research concern. This author wishes to emphasize for all Myanmar Christians the need for Christian mission that preserves the missional church consisting in a fellowship with Christ, that proclaims the gospel, conducts worship services, and serves those in need. Therefore, this research intention is in line with the Lausanne Covenant of 1974 that reads:

> We affirmed that there is only one Savior and only one Gospel, although there is a wide diversity of evangelistic approaches . . . we also reject as derogatory to Christ and the Gospel every kind of syncretism and dialogue which implies that Christ speaks equally through all religions and ideologies. Jesus Christ, being himself the only God-man, who gave himself as the only ransom for sinners, is the only mediator between God and man. There is no other name by which we must be saved.[20]

---

17. Schulz, *Mission from the Cross*, 87.
18. Newbigin, *One Body*, 42.
19. Newbigin, *Open Secret*, 19.
20. Snyder, *Global Good News*, 43.

If proclamation no longer calls out people to repentance and conversion, through which they are connected to the church, then the sense of a missional church is lost. For a missional church is one that has emerged as a result of the salvific activities of God's mission and then passes the mission of God on to others through proclaiming the Word. This understanding agrees already with one of the first modern missiologists, Gisbertus Voetius (1589–1676), who insists that the goal of the theology of mission is for the conversion of unbelievers and the establishment of churches.[21]

Assumption and Presupposition

The people of Myanmar are still held together in the primal religion, Burmese Nat worship. It is evident that their socioeconomic and religiopolitical life are deeply entwined with ideas, concepts, beliefs and practices of Nat worship. Moreover, the Western missionaries came into the country along with colonialism during the same era, and they were one and the same in the eyes of the people. Therefore, the native people preserved the primal religio-culture called Burmese Nat worship as a tool to resist the influence of the Western culture. While some Western missionaries and colonists treated the indigenous culture as primitive and pagan, other missionaries were drawn to the cultural elements as a necessary tool for doing mission work. In the same vein, culture becomes a necessary tool for the local people to resist the colonial system because colonialism is considered a threat to primal religious and cultural practices.[22]

As Christians we are members of two kingdoms, that of the world and the one of heaven. Andrew Walls suggests taking the Christian faith and finding a local expression to live as a Christian while yet a member of one's society.[23] Thus, Christian missiologists, theologians, and ministers need to respond with the gospel to convert the people and transform the society they live in. The researcher hopes in this study that the gospel be preached and accepted so that the primal religion, Nat worship, will be transformed by the Christian faith, not vice versa.

---

21. Boston University, "Voetius, Gisbertus."
22. Ott and Netland, *Globalizing Theology*, 97.
23. Walls, *Missionary Movement*, 7.

Introduction, Missiological Problem, and Rationale

In his book, *Anthropology for Christian Witness*, Charles Kraft writes:

> We must maintain that people are saved or lost on the basis of whether or not their primary commitment is to the true God. Whatever the secondary allegiances, rituals, other beliefs and practices may be they are all of much less importance than the central issue of primary allegiance. Many of those customs will be changed in the process of Christian growth, as with the Hebrews, but God is still very patient with secondary things.[24]

The main idea Kraft presented here lies at the heart of a Christian hope that the old customs are being transformed in the process of Christian growth. The attitude of contemporary Christian theologians needs to be informed and transformed as they attempt to utilize elements from previous religious practice as a tool for doing Christian mission in Myanmar. The researcher presumes that utilizing Nat worship principles such as rituals and customs can be perilous to the Christian faith because Nat worship principles tend to transform the Christian faith. The responsibilities of a Christian missionary are to define the mission of God based on the Scripture rather than the rituals and customs of the people.

The socioeconomic and religiopolitical life of the Burmese people are closely knit together in the primal religion, so forsaking Nat worship is to abandon the source of life. Instead of abandoning the former rituals and customs, the contemporary Myanmar theologians shifted their missiological approach by using the customs of Nat worship for Christian mission. This shift in approach misses the most important aspect of Christian mission, the soteriological dimension in the mission of God.

This is an urgent and much needed task, because until now the Buddhist karma has no alternative explanation for suffering and the use of Nat worship principles has found no alternative explanation for escaping human suffering. This is an opportunity for Christian theologians to impose the concept of salvation in the explanation of suffering because salvation in Christian mission is the backbone. The good news is that Jesus Christ has suffered on the cross for humanity 2000 years ago.

---

24. Kraft, *Anthropology for Christian Witness*, 211.

The researcher's presupposition is that the *missio Christi* is a legitimate response to the Buddhist explanation of human suffering in the Burmese context. The Nat worship principles stand in opposition to the Christian approach toward suffering. On the one hand, the Nat worshipers' solution for suffering is pleasing Nat spirits by feeding them raw meat prepared in the sacrificial offering so that the wishes of the shaman, sorcerer, and astrologist would be heard and granted and, on the other hand, the Christian's solution for suffering is to accept the crucified Christ. The former has to give while the latter has to receive it.

For Christian mission, the Burmese people who engage in this worship and practice need to be freed from it in order to find peace and comfort in Christ and his suffering on the cross. For, it is at the cross where humanity should define its own reality and who God is in their lives. Therefore, a detailed concept of suffering and its causes among the Burmese people will be explored more fully in this study with special reference to the suffering of Christ on the cross that is brought forth in the proclamation of the gospel in the church. For a mission theology within the context of Myanmar, it becomes a *sine qua non* for establishing a Christocentric and an ecclesiocentric mission.

Missiologically speaking, Buddhism and Nat worship take an anti-Christian stance. For example, Burmese Buddhism is an atheistic system that rejects the existence of a personal God, and Nat worship is a true expression of that atheism. It is pagan in nature by worshiping evil spirits. There are three reasons explaining why the Burmese Buddhists constantly feel threatened by the Christian mission: (1) Christian missionaries came along with the British colonialists that Burmese people conceived to be one and the same. (2) The concept of Burmese Nat is deeply rooted in the socioeconomic and religiopolitical life of the people. As a result, for anyone who converts, becoming a Christian means leaving their source of life. (3) The missiological message is treated as alien to the Burmese context.

Christianity came to Myanmar in three layers: (1) it came with a foreign language, English, (2) it is wrapped in a foreign culture, and (3) it came with foreign images. In response to these three layers, U Nu, the former prime minister of Myanmar, promulgated Buddhism as a State religion in 1961 to be integrated nationwide in its culture – Nat worship principles – and assumed as the dominant religion for Myanmar.[25] Therefore, Burmese Buddhists rejected the Christian faith on the grounds that it is alien and inappropriate for their practical life.

A notable Myanmar Christian theologian, Simon Pau Khan En, published his doctoral dissertation under the title *Nat Worship: A Paradigm for Doing Contextual Theology in Myanmar*, which gives a perspective on Burmese Nat worship as an essential component for doing the mission of God in Myanmar.[26] He concludes that conversion does not necessarily mean to identify with Christianity and the church.[27] In response to this, the present researcher mainly uses *missio Dei* with specific focus on *missio Christi* and *ecclesiae* to argue what it means to be an authentic Christian in the context of Burmese Nat worship. Along the way, the researcher revisits the mission work of Adoniram Judson to make a case, and explores the interaction between the Christian mission brought about by the Western missionaries and the Burmese Nat worship in a pluralistic setting.

A serious study of this problem is long overdue, but it must develop a relevant missiological approach to Burmese Nat worship which will address the present reality by taking seriously the *missio Christi* and *ecclesiae* for the conversion of the Burmese people. The following three considerations are taken into account: First, Burmese primal religion (Nat worship) and cultural elements are introduced with a concise interpretation. Second, this study explores how, as a result of the Burmese Nat worship influence, Burmese Christian society was changed into a looser group, which allowed for the infusion of alien religious forces. On the one hand, liberal Christianity creates space for the infiltration of Nat worship into Christianity. On the other, liberal Christian leaders started to develop the idea that all religions – Buddhism, Christianity, Hinduism and Islam – lead to the same destination.[28] Third, the author outlines by accommodating *missio Christi* and *ecclesiae* for the rediscovery of the mission of God through the suffering of Christ on the

---

25. Sakhong, *In Defense of Identity*, 12.
26. En, *Nat Worship*, 8.
27. En, "Quest for Authentic Myanmar," 84.
28. Yong, *Missiological Spirit*, 56.

cross. The cross is where the wrath of God and the love of God meet in order to produce the gospel.[29]

Given these disparities, the Burmese Buddhists are blind because of their atheistic worldview and cannot see the suffering of Christ as a ransom for many. The contemporary Myanmar Christians' approach to Burmese Nat worship is irrelevant and false because the role of Christ and the church have been largely marginalized or compromised which has resulted in a lack of clarity and understanding of the gospel of Christ. For instance, Myanmar liberal Christians rejected using the phrase, "Jesus is the only way" in the midst of Burmese Buddhists because, they said, it is too exclusive.[30] Thus, the researcher's assumption is that reclaiming the role of Christ and the role of the church will be a response to the Burmese way of wanting to escape from human suffering here and now and the hereafter. This missiological assumption is to re-root the gospel of Christ and re-establish a missional church for the fulfilment of the mission of God. Against the inappropriate and unnecessary religio-cultural elements that stem from Burmese Nat worship, this study argues the proclamation of the gospel of Christ for the conversion of the people and the establishment of churches.

Research Concern

There are two main research concerns. The first research concern is that Nat worship has been recognized by Myanmar liberal theologians as instrumental for Christian mission. For this reason, the researcher is making a case for Christian mission in response to the contemporary Christianity in Myanmar. The theology of Christian mission in the context of Myanmar needs to be redefined, as Christopher Wright asserts, the Bible is the basis of all forms of practical theology, including missiology. The mission of God is not to reconcile with spirit worship and idolatry but to fulfill the Great Commission of Christ and to "make disciples of all nations (Matthew 28:19–20)."[31] This is the first concern of the research.

---

29. Katimori, *Pain of God*, 21.
30. En, *Nat Worship*, 268.
31. Wright, *Mission of God*, 21.

Initial restrictions to Christian mission work were imposed in 1962 and strengthened by the subsequent Burmese military coups in 1988, 1997, 2007, and 2021. Myanmar has 55 million people with 87.9 percent Buddhists, 6.2 percent Christians, 4.3 percent Muslims, 0.8 percent Animists, 0.5 percent Hindus, 0.2 percent others, and 0.1 percent none.[32] Moreover, the Myanmar ethnic majority favors Burmese Buddhism, and the ethnic minority follows Christianity. Christianity in Myanmar has, therefore, survived ruthless suppression for over the last fifty years. In addition, the multiethnicity and religious pluralistic society of the country creates division, hatred, and discrimination everywhere. Especially, religious interview is very sensitive and risky in the Buddhist society in Myanmar.

Therefore, the researcher aims at a minimum of ten persons for interview and survey due to difficult access to the potential interviewees. The data obtained from the potential interviewees will be examined to identify two pressing issues. First, the interview responses from Burmese Buddhists will clarify the distinction between Buddhism and Nat worship in their daily life. Second, the interview responses from Myanmar Christian leaders will demonstrate their perspectives on the relationship between Christianity and Nat worship.

The data will be analyzed to tease out their missiological standpoint toward the Burmese Nat worship and Burmese Buddhism. Then, the researcher will draw a legitimate statement for Christian mission from the Scripture and a Trinitarian *missio Dei* geared toward responding to Myanmar Christianity.

The identification of Burmese Buddhism with the social and cultural identity of being Burmese has been a significant factor in Burmese nationalism since the postcolonial period. Officials proudly announced, "We Burmese are Buddhists," since 1910. The identity of Myanmar ethnicity with Theravada Buddhist authority was already central in the hegemonic discourse of pre-colonial polities.[33] Since 1961, U Nu, then prime minister, had made Buddhism the state religion of the country, which reinforced religious power to control the secular world in Myanmar.

---

32. https://joshuaproject.net/countries/bm, accessed on 20 October 2022.
33. Schober, *Modern Buddhist Conjunctures*, 2.

Missiological Rationale

The missiological rationale for this research is the syncretism of Myanmar Christian mission in the context of Burmese Nat worship. This research insists that the mission of God is grounded on the Scriptures so that emerging Christian leaders, ministers, and theologians must mitigate the influence of Burmese Nat worship in Christian mission.

For this reason, the research findings will construe the Christian mission rooted in the Trinitarian *missio Dei*.[34] This research will help to look beyond and discern the divine mission of God beckoning man to return to him. There are two misconceptions for the Christian missions in Myanmar. First, Burmese Buddhists saw American Baptist missionaries more as partners with colonialism than as religious teachers. To a degree there is some truth in that association. For even the most devoted foreign missionary, Judson, once said, "to be successful in Christian mission among the Burmese people, to occupy their country is the best way."[35] As a result, the liberal Christians conceived that because the Burmese Buddhists saw Christianity as pro-colonialism rather than as a religion, it is appropriate to use Burmese Nat worship to indigenize Christianity in Myanmar. [36]

The church is an institution bound by the mandate of Jesus Christ, that is, to preach the gospel to the heathen. In the strict sense of the term, the church shall have one history, "the church as the body of Christ is a living organism, for from the head the whole body is assembled, and one member hangs onto the next through the joints."[37] The mission of God and the activities of human organization need a clear demarcation. For instance, the American missionary, Judson, should not be associated with the British colonialists because the mission of God and the colonialists have no common goal. Judson quickly realized the mission of God is solely to preach the gospel, therefore, he quit as a translator for the British colonialists. In line with this statement, Richard Niebuhr observes that Christianity is a way of life, and it should be separated from human culture.[38]

---

34. Rogers, *Basic Introduction to Missions*, 17.
35. Nyunt, *Mission amidst Pagodas*, 50.
36. En, "Nat Worship," 170.
37. Petri, *Mission and Church*.
38. Niebuhr, *Christ and Culture*, 49.

Second, it was previously mentioned that the word of God came to Myanmar in three stages. In reaction to the above three stages, U Ne Win (1962–88), then prime minister of Myanmar, renewed Burmese Buddhist-Nat worship with the claim that it meets all human needs in Myanmar. This multidimensional need of the people includes the socioeconomic and religiopolitical spheres. As a result, Christians in Myanmar are under the influence of Burmese Nat worship. It is essential that the gospel of Christ meets the multidimensional need of the people without blending colonialism and Nat worship.

Simon Pau Khan En, formerly a professor at the Myanmar Institute of Theology and currently an Emeritus Pastor of the Tedim Baptist Church-Yangon, explores the concept of Christian mission in Myanmar. En writes:

> To become an authentic and significant Christian minority in the country of Myanmar, the present researcher discovered that the churches should no longer remain lethargic but should attempt a more relevant and dynamic theology which will be constructive to the churches, the society and the State as well. Christians need a more relevant political theology to empower them to involve themselves in the socio-political realities of the country.[39]

The political theology should not be the undergirding foundation for the mission of God. The researcher views that such cultural and political elements serve as instruments which do not help the fulfillment of the mission of God.[40] The Trinitarian *missio Dei* should be the undergirding foundation for the mission of God. U Kyaw Than, a Burmese theologian, once said at the conference of the International Missionary Council held in Ghana in 1957, "After all, we need to be reminded over and over again that mission is Christ's and not ours."[41] He writes:

> Since the Christian mission is much larger than missions as such, it would be unfair to become completely preoccupied with missions every time we talk about the Christian mission in Asia,

---

39. En, *Nat Worship*, 12.
40. Elliston, *Missiological Research Design*, 5.
41. Than, "What Mission Is," 441.

> Africa, or Latin America. At the same time, without being preoccupied only with missions as such, it should be possible, in considering the Christian mission in Asia to limit our thoughts, for the present purpose, to the matter of the proclamation of Christ to the unchurched or to the witness of the Church to those outside her life, rather than taking up everything that can possibly be included under the title, "The Christian mission in Asia to-day."[42]

Notwithstanding his Burmese background, U Kyaw Than points out that Christians are members of the *missio ecclesia* started by Christ and it is not that "we started a club of our own with a constitution drawn up by mutual consent to fulfill an agreed purpose."[43] Rather than attempting to reconcile Nat worship with Christianity, U Kyaw Than suggests that Christian mission should operate within the framework of the Trinitarian *missio Dei*. He asserts, "We are enlisted in the Spirit-led mission."[44] The ultimate purpose of Christian mission is for the conversion of people by the proclamation of the gospel of Jesus Christ. Another contemporary Myanmar theologian, Khawsiama, introduces the concept of salvation. He writes:

> For Christians, the Christ-event is significant in salvation history. It opens our eyes to see Jesus as Savior and Liberator and his salvation as liberation in the Buddhist cultural context. For Buddhists, the term "Liberator" is more valuable than "Savior." Gautama Buddha is not a savior, but the enlightened one who found and showed the Way of Liberation. The work of the savior is to save the whole life of a human being–body, mind, and soul. Moreover, Christian salvation may be from a variety of situations: from enemies (Exod 14:14; 1 Sam 14:45).[45]

The usage of the term liberation by Khawsiama is more of a reflection and an experience for Myanmar people in the process of the military oppression than salvation from a biblical point of view. Assimilating the concepts of

---

42. Than, "Christian Mission in Asia," 154.
43. Than, *What Mission Is*, 440.
44. Than, *What Mission Is*, 441.
45. Khawsiama, "Jesus Christ," 188.

liberation and salvation in an unjust and violent society can be a challenging question to answer from a missiological point of view. However, the purpose of this research is not to elaborate the concept of liberation and salvation from the perspective of social justice and human liberation. It is rather to understand the mission of God in relation to the syncretism of some Christians.

Because of the church-state relationship and the political upheaval in addition to the recent military coup, mission activities in Myanmar have been redefined. Hence, contemporary Christian theologians in Myanmar were vacillating between the concept of salvation from eternal death and liberation from the military oppression. In line with this, Saw Hlaing Bwa, a Burmese Christian professor at the Myanmar Institute of Theology writes:

> God's self-disclosure, according to Christian understanding, has been discerned and reflected in the Bible in the context of the Israelite people and continued in the western European context, African context, Latin American context, Asian context. It is therefore not sufficient to discern and reflect God's self-disclosure only in and out of our scripture, traditions in isolation from world history. Theology should be re-interpreted, re-rooted and refreshed alive from the perspective of the life and experience of the people in every turn of history and engaged in the religious thought as well as the struggle of the suffering people, a theology that empowers the people for full humanity.[46]

Due to the bifurcation of inclusivism and exclusivism, Western missionaries are accused of imposing their cultural elements on those to whom they go to serve in the mission field. Therefore, Simon Pau Khan En argues that "the churches in Myanmar are not the churches of Myanmar, but just the replicas (Xerox copy) and potted plants of the western churches, both in their thinking and structure."[47] The missiological problem is the gulf between the left-wing and the right-wing theological standpoint in the multifaceted religious settings in Myanmar. Simon Pau Khan En suggests that, in order for the churches in Myanmar to become churches of Myanmar, "the basic theological problem for Burmese Christian theology is not that which is concerned with

---

46. Bwa, "Challenges of Change."
47. En, *Quest for Authentic Myanmar*, 41.

the bottle, but that which concerns the 'wine' itself."[48] The question is, how can the gospel that is brought by foreign people with foreign languages and foreign images get rooted in the soil of Myanmar?

Simon Pau Khan En thinks the indigenous religio-cultures are compatible with the word of God. As he has pointed out, "This is neither to venerate nor to romanticize any particular culture for every culture has its merits and demerits." However, the researcher argues that religio-cultural elements cannot be the tool to measure the truth. Religion cannot be claimed as the remedy for human suffering because when it is, as John Lennox has rightly pointed out, "when anyone appears to claim that religion is the remedy for human race's faults, to many people, must be, to say the least, problematical, if not altogether incredible."[49] Rather, religion has been the cause of conflict and chaos in the world.

While Burmese liberal theologians have attempted to bring in the religio-cultural elements or Nat worship as the remedy for the problem of human suffering, the present researcher proposes the Trinitarian *missio Dei* with special focus on the *missio Christi* and *ecclesiae* as the legitimate explanation for human suffering. When the concept of the Trinitarian *missio Dei* grounded in the Scripture is not properly applied, Christian mission will not survive the test of other religions and it will distort the gospel of Christ. The mission of God is a *"divinely appointed mission"* which cannot be twisted by human services.[50]

Revisiting the work of Judson in the Burmese Nat context gives a fresh reflection on the true nature of the mission of Christ and his church within Burmese Buddhist society.[51] For example, naming God as the eternal Being and the *zayat* ministry as a missional church within the Burmese society plays a crucial role for the mission of God today. When Judson was asked, "who is Jesus,?" by a Burman, he replied, "He is a being without beginning or end, who is not subject of old age and death, but always is."[52] Judson did not believe that Christianity should follow the Western civilization as he refrained

---

48. Elwood, ed., *What Asian Christians*, 89.
49. Gooding and Lennox, *Claiming to Answer*, 43.
50. Elliston, *Missiological Research Design*, 5.
51. Harvey, *History of Burma*, 139.
52. Judson, *Life of Adoniram Judson*, 110.

from teaching the arts and sciences of the Western world.[53] By addressing the role of Christ and the church, this study will distinguish the uniqueness of Christ and the church from the Burmese Nat worship. In the second place, the use of an indigenous religious structure, the Nat worship principle, will be contrasted with the biblical truth claim.

The biblical truth claim implies that there is only one God and that he sent his Son Jesus Christ to bring the gospel. In other words, it is an exclusive claim that there is no other gospel except the one springing from the cross. Along the way, the practice of Nat worship in relation to their socioeconomic and religiopolitical life will be tested whether or not it really gives benefit to the practitioners. Myanmar liberal theologians constantly feel threatened by the emerging radical Burmese Buddhism; hence they opted for syncretism for doing Christian mission in a pluralistic society. The gospel, the main content in the mission of God, does not come from a cultural vacuum; it came through a very painful path that authentic Christians must follow in witnessing to the world.

En asserts, "Nat worship enriches the Christian message and will serve as an effective source and a paradigm for fashioning ecumenical theology for Myanmar." He adds, "Christians in Myanmar today have to learn the theology of human nature relationship from Nat worship."[54] The Burmese language and customs are largely infused with Buddhist and Nat ideas and ways. In other words, the gospel that Adoniram Judson implanted two hundred years ago has been reversed by the Burmese Buddhist regimes.

Leslie Newbigin observes that the mission of God is incomplete without a clear understanding of who Jesus is.[55] The most pressing issue facing the mission of God in Myanmar is how the Burmese see Jesus Christ as Savior and Lord – not just liberator – in the Burmese Buddhist context. Jesus, the second person of the Trinity, must be treated as the authority that guides Christian mission. The mission of God is fully accomplished by Jesus Christ on the cross, therefore, the *missio Christi* gave birth to the church. Similarly, Georg Vicedom puts church as the vehicle of mission.[56] By assimilating Christ

---

53. Judson, *Life of Adoniram Judson*, 82.
54. En, "Nat Worship," 1, 50.
55. Schulz, *Mission from the Cross*, 91. See also Newbigin, *Open Secret*, 171.
56. Vicedom, *Mission of God*, 15.

with Nat (Devil spirits) one distorts the divine nature of Christ, a serious problem for the Trinitarian *missio Dei*. The present researcher attempts to respond to Burmese Nat worship with the question of "who is Jesus for the Burmese people?" The divine attribution of Christ cannot be downgraded to equate it with an avatar or the Buddha. The true answer to this question should not be determined by one's religious affiliation, for example, for a Hindu, he would be an avatar, for the Buddhist, he is the Buddha and for the Muslim, he is Muhammed, the messenger of God.[57]

The correct answer has to be proven by the truth claim in Scripture. If Jesus is seen as an avatar for the Hindu, then there must be many Jesuses because there are many avatars. Whether Jesus is conceived as liberator or savior, his relationship to the Father and the Holy Spirit must guide Christian mission. When Jesus Christ is not presented and taught clearly, the church is corrupting its message and becomes non-missionary in its approach.[58]

God's mission is fulfilled through the suffering of Jesus on the cross which serves as the only reason for God's redemption and reconciliation to the sinful world. The cross is where God's love is revealed to us and that heals our wounds. In other words, the cross is where both the wrath of God and the love of God are revealed. The cross brings together God's rejection of the world's sin and his unconditional love for all sinful human beings.[59]

The core message of the mission of God is that salvation is meant for all people, and it springs from the cross and suffering of Jesus Christ. This theology of mission that focuses and defines the *missio Christi* will qualify and correct the Burmese Nat worship principle for Myanmar. Christians in Myanmar must reclaim the true nature of Jesus Christ as the only Savior and his church as a locus of witness for the gospel of Jesus Christ.

The Research Problem

The context to prove in this research is that contemporary Myanmar Christian theologians have distorted the traditional meaning of the mission of God by employing Nat worship principles for Christian mission. This is the main

---

57. Al-Yahsubi, *Muhammad Messenger of Allah*, 6.
58. Flett, *Witness of God*, 72.
59. Kitamori, *Theology*, 20.

motivation for the research questions addressed in the next section. There is one research problem in this study – How do the contemporary Christian theologians understand the mission of God in the context of Burmese Buddhist-Nat worship? Their understanding of the mission of God is compromising with the traditional religion and Buddhism. Addressing this research problem encompasses all the research questions along with subsequent operational questions. We will return to this reference in the next section.

There are two reasons for the research problem. First, because Christianity came into the country along with colonialism, the indigenous people perceived they were one and the same group. This resulted in liberal Christianity embracing Burmese Nat worship principles as essential components for Christian mission in Myanmar. Therefore, the liberals and Nat worshipers perceived Christians as intruders of the indigenous religion, and they were regarded as a political tool for the expansion of Western culture and colonial activities. A Myanmar theologian, Ciin Sian Khai, provokingly said, "During the colonial period, Buddhism weakened because the British government ceased to be the defender and promoter of the Buddhist faith and Christianity came into the country with guns and swords."[60]

The second reason is the result of the first. Christians are regarded as traitors, aliens, and second-class citizens in Myanmar. On the one hand, the ethnic majority Burmese are connected with the majority religion, Buddhism, and on the other, the ethnic minorities – Chin, Kachin, Karenni, and Karen are connected with the minority religion, Christianity, in the country. Interestingly, the Burmese are the majority in ethnicity and religion, Buddhism, and the Chin, Kachin, Karenni, and Karen are the minority in ethnicity and religion, Christianity.[61] Although the American Baptist missionaries arrived to the ethnic minorities one hundred years after the ethnic majority, the ethnic minorities who previously followed a primal religion experienced a mass movement toward the Christian faith.[62]

Prime Minister U Nu expelled all foreigners including missionaries from the country in 1962 as a reaction to the influence of colonialism and Christian expansion from the West, and reinforced the identification of Buddhism

---

60. Khai, *Rediscovering*, 1.
61. Dorp, *Ethnic Diversity*, 22.
62. Cing, *Tedim Gam*, 66.

with Burmese nationalism. In other words, a handful of Christians (6.2%) in Myanmar have to live among people for whom the word Burmese or Burma is synonymous with Buddhist (87.9%). Burmese language and customs are deeply infused with Buddhist ideas and ways and many animistic (Nat worship) elements.

As the result of constant suppressions from all dimensional aspects, Christian theologians in Myanmar are encumbered under the influence of Burmese Buddhism. To make matters worse, Myanmar went through extreme socioeconomic hardship and religiopolitical crisis since the military coup in 1962, and the Burmese Nat worship principles were strengthened because they provided alternative explanations for the suffering of the people. This association of Nat worship with Buddhism impedes the penetration of the gospel. Hence, the greatest challenge which Myanmar Christians are facing today is to ensure that the people clearly hear and understand the gospel in the Myanmar context. Though the Buddha taught men to rely upon themselves in order to achieve their own salvation, the Burmese Buddhists still employ Nat worship principles to avoid or diminish all kinds of suffering because they failed to achieve salvation.[63] In light of this, the contemporary Myanmar theologians developed a new missiological methodology for reaching out to the Burmese people by embracing Nat worship principles. When individuals convert to the Christian faith, the syncretism of Christianity and Nat worship entails a different worldview than that of the traditional Christianity.

Consequently, in the course of their faith journey Christians in Myanmar are faced with an identity crisis that is exacerbated by additional pressure from communities to stay true to their roots and traditional values. The approaches adopted by previous missionaries and contemporary theologians will be later analyzed from a missiological and biblical point of view.[64] If the mission of God is to succeed in contexts where people are bound by traditional religions such as Nat worship, missionaries have to pay attention to the needs of the people and at the same time remain faithful to Scripture.

The intention of this dissertation is to respond to the contemporary Myanmar theologians' understanding of the mission of God and to assess their attempt to reconcile Nat worship with Christianity. The researcher

---

63. King, *Buddhism and Christianity*, 19–20.
64. Bailey, *Adoniram Judson*, 61. See also Chapter 2, section "God in Myanmar."

argues that the gospel of Christ is to transform Burmese Nat worship and the life of the people but not that the gospel has to be influenced by Nat worship. The missiological approaches in this research would best serve the needs of the church, and they would at the same time ensure that the gospel is not compromised with Nat worship principles, especially in the attempt to answer legitimate questions about human suffering in the Burmese Nat-Buddhist context.

Limitation and Delimitation

With regard to limitation of the research, it should be mentioned that many historiographies and biographies of previous missionaries are not available due to many circumstances in the country. The present researcher will try his best to cope with this limitation by using all possible means. It is, therefore, important to highlight the limitation and delimitation in this work.

First, the limitation in this research work is caused by the unstable political situation since 1962 that brought about a shortage of scholarly work in all fields because the country was closed and it was no longer possible for foreigners to undertake field research work, as Melford Spiro has noted.[65] As no foreign missionaries and expatriates could come to the country for any professional work, there are no competent national missionaries and theologians in the country at this time, so there are limitations in the current research work. Another limitation in terms of resources is impeded by the multiethnic groups in Myanmar, as Stevenson noted in the following.

This study is limited by a current political crisis that prevents fieldwork in the entire country of Myanmar. As a result of the recent Burmese military crackdown that brutally killed over two thousand civilians and arrested over ten thousand within eighteen months, Myanmar has become one of the top five most dangerous countries to travel in 2022. The military coup in February 2021 had a negative impact as so many church buildings have been burned, destroyed, and looted in Kayah, Chin, Kachin, and Sagaing states in Myanmar.[66] As a result, church services in those areas use Zoom meetings due to the COVID-19 pandemic and the coup. However, internet services

---

65. Spiro, *Burmese Supernaturalism*, 9.
66. Hmung, "After 2021 Military Coup," 19–23.

were cut off in hilly regions. Missiological fieldwork such as interview and participant observation are still prohibited until further notice.

H. C. Stevenson writes, "Myanmar is a melting pot of racial groups, and this multiplicity of ethnics groups produced difficulties for any researcher wanting to cover the religious beliefs of all ethnic groups."[67] As a result, the current research focuses on the Burmese Nat worship and Christianity regardless of the 135 different racial groups. The final limitation in the present research work is caused by the current political crisis due to the military coup in February 2021 that prohibited missiological fieldwork until further notification. Therefore, personal interviews with religious leaders in the country is impossible. The researcher will cope with the problem by email correspondence and personal interviews with Burmese immigrants in the states.

In terms of delimitation, this research will address the Burmese Nat worship principles in relation to Burmese Buddhism which is deeply interwoven with the socioeconomic and religiopolitical life. Myanmar is not only a multiethnic but also a religiously pluralistic society where world religions, Buddhism, Hinduism, Islam, and Christianity have coexisted for centuries. Although this study is related to religious syncretism, it is impossible to include Christian syncretistic practices with Hinduism and Islam. Moreover, the researcher has briefly surveyed Burmese Nat worship principles which the contemporary Christian theologians apply in doing theology in the country. In other words, while it is impossible to deal with all the tenets of Nat worship and Burmese Buddhism, the researcher will attempt to demonstrate the elements of Nat worship which are compromising with Christian practices.

As the primary aim of this research is a response to the contribution of Nat worship to Christian mission proposed by contemporary Myanmar theologians, the researcher argues on the ground of the Trinitarian *missio Dei* in the Scriptures. Two crucial issues that emerge from this research work are *missio Christi* and *missio ecclesiae*. These will be the demarcation between Nat worship and Christianity. The former describes the source of salvation, and the latter indicates the locus of proclaiming the gospel of Christ.

---

67. Stevenson, *Hill Peoples of Burma*, 5.

Research Questions

The purpose of this section is to identify the problem which the contemporary Myanmar Christian theologians have created by compromising their position with the Burmese traditional religion. Each major research question has three subsequent operational questions as a part of it. The interview questions helped the researcher in finding why Buddhism, Christianity, and the primal religion, Nat worship have continued to be the subject of debate among the Myanmar Christians. The following questions deserve attention in order to understand the pervasiveness of Nat worship in Myanmar.

Research Question 1: How ubiquitous is the Burmese primal religion (Nat Worship) in Myanmar?

Operational Question 1.1: How prevalent is the Burmese Nat worship and Burmese Buddhism in their sociocultural and religiopolitical life?

Operational Question 1.2: How does the Burmese Nat worship inform everyday life among the Burmese Buddhists and Christians in Myanmar?

Operational Question 1.3: What is the impact of the Burmese Nat worship on the Christian churches in Myanmar?

Research question 1 and its subsequent operational questions aim at describing the pervasiveness of the Burmese Nat worship and its influence on the sociocultural and religiopolitical life of the people. The Burmese Buddhist-Nat worship involves 87.9 percent of the country, whereas all other influences are far below that: 6.2 percent Christianity, 4.3 percent Islam, 0.8 percent Animists, 0.5 percent Hindus , 0.2 percent others, and 0.1 percent none.[68] This research question and the subsequent operational questions aim also at finding out more about how the Burmese traditional religion informs their sociocultural and religiopolitical life.

In addition, research question 1 aims at discovering how the Burmese traditional religion impacts their everyday life. Research question 1 is an important part of the study because it explores the prevalence of Burmese Buddhist-Nat worship in the society. It is important to understand Nat worship first and then approach it missiologically so that the mission of God would relate to the sociocultural and religiopolitical realities of the Burmese people and transform them into the kingdom of God.

---

68. "Burma People 2020." https://theodora.com/wfbcurrent/burma/burma/_people.html, accessed on 9 June 2021.

Research Question 2: How does Nat worship contrast with a Trinitarian theology?

Operational Question 2:1: How does the concept of God in Nat worship contrast with Trinitarian worship?

Operational Question 2:2: How does the concept of salvation in Nat worship contrast with salvation in Christ alone?

Operational Question 2:3: How does the role of spirit in Nat worship contrast with the work of the Holy Spirit?

This study claims that the sociocultural and religiopolitical life of the Burmese is predominantly influenced by the Buddhist-Nat worship, specifically the supernatural power of the Nat. Hence, the research question and its subsequent questions examine how a Trinitarian God is received in Myanmar's society in light of the supernaturalism. This research question and the operational questions are important in determining how much the mission of God is anchored to the triune God and why the Burmese Nat worship principles invisibly permeate even among Christians in Myanmar.

The Burmese Nat worship principles will be examined and compared in light of the Trinitarian *missio Dei* framework, as well as the notion of suffering and salvation based on the redemptive work of Jesus Christ.

Research Question 3: What role does the church play in the context of Burmese Nat worship?

Operational Question 3:1: How can the Myanmar churches respond to the two-tiered Christians, who became Christians but go back to previous practices in order to meet their temporary need?

Operational Question 3:2: How can the mission of the church effectively engage with the mission field in the context of Burmese Nat worship?

Operational Question 3:3: How can the church address the needs of the everyday life of Christians in the context of Burmese Nat worship?

Missiologists have done tremendous groundbreaking work on how the church responds to the challenge of ancestor worship, spirit worship, and indigenous religious practices. Research question 3 and its operational questions intend to explore the question of the conversion of the Burmese Nat worshipers through the proclamation of the gospel of Christ in the church. This research question will identify the significant meaning of conversion and discuss the dual allegiances of Burmese Nat and Christian beliefs, a syncretism of two religious systems. In other words, some of these Christians go back to their previous practices whenever they meet daily problems such as illness, misfortune, drought, marriage, and failure in business.

This question traces some solutions for a missiological approach that seeks to transform the worldview of Nat worship in order to prevent these Christians with dual allegiances from going back to their previous religious rituals.

Preliminary Research Approach/Method

The researcher focuses on qualitative research because this approach allows multiple systems including case study, historical analysis, ethnographic interviewing, and participant observation.[69] More specifically, the researcher adopts two methods, namely, the historical method and ethnographic research method to strengthen the research work. The intention of this section is to address the research problem and the research questions by employing relevant research methods.

The historical research gathers the necessary and relevant historical data needed in this study. Since the primary purpose of this study is Christian mission in the context of Burmese Nat-Buddhist worship in Myanmar, the researcher adopts a historical method to collect data from the past.

Historical research entails more than simply data gathering and presenting factual information; its profound effectiveness is the ability to interpret the data. Sometimes it requires reinterpreting previous historical events by revisiting existing understandings and replacing them with new concepts which are essential for understanding our modern society. To understand and interpret the complex relationship between Burmese Buddhism and Christianity, it is necessary to learn from the past events and history, and interpret for the future. Therefore, a historical research method is essential in this study.

The ethnographic approach is based on personal observations, informal interviews, and casual survey in collecting relevant data. It involves investigation of the traditional religious culture that has a primary concern for the concept of a supreme being, and this approach has a biblical missiological concern as well, that is, about crossing barriers with the gospel.[70]

---

69. Elliston, *Missiological Research Design*, 7.
70. Bradshaw, *Change across Cultures*, 98.

To address the research problem, the present researcher employs qualitative research that typically studies a relatively small number of individuals or situations and preserves the individuality of each of these in the analyses, rather than collecting data from large samples and spreading the data across individuals or situations.[71] Subsequently, the researcher makes a brief survey on the relationship between Nat worship and Burmese Buddhism as well as the contemporary Christian theologians' view toward the Burmese Nat-Buddhists. Henceforth, the scope of the study will be narrowed down to the Burmese community in Myanmar.

There are two possible sources in this approach: primary and secondary sources. The primary sources are the original work of the persons studied, such as the writings of Adoniram Judson and his son, Edward Judson. These sources also include the European Roman Catholic missionaries, Vincentius Sangermano, Gaspar De Cruz, Bomferrus,[72] and Christian merchants, Marco Polo and Philip de Brito, who came to Myanmar from the sixteenth to the twentieth centuries.[73]

By interpreting and analyzing the history of foreign missionaries in the past and the contemporary Myanmar theologians' work, the researcher hopes to find how future Christian missionaries and ministers of the church should approach adherents of Nat worship and respond to the Myanmar liberal Christians who have broken away from traditional missionary work. This study aims to demonstrate the elements of Nat worship which contemporary Myanmar liberal theologians employ that are incompatible with the mission of God. In order to learn why contemporary Myanmar Christian theologians utilize the elements of Nat worship and how they view it, historical research and interviews will be conducted.

The second ethnographic research method, as previously mentioned, is based on a casual interview and survey that will hopefully help the researcher to identify and analyze unexpected and expected views, aspects, and issues. More importantly, the ethnographic studies can help in discovering the worldview of the targeted audience that is very important in this study.[74]

---

71. Bickman and Rog, *Applied Research Methods*, 75.
72. Coupland, *British Empire History*, 51.
73. Harvey, *History of Burma*, 186–87. See also Aung, *History of Burma*, 137–39.
74. Elliston, *Missiological Research Design*, 35.

Coding and interpreting ethnographic research data can be a daunting task depending on the size of interview questions, data collections, fieldnotes, and transcripts. Due to the unforeseeable restrictions in Myanmar since the military coup in February 2021, the researcher decided to conduct a brief survey which may be useful in discovering the contemporary worldview of Burmese Buddhist Nat worship. The interview survey helps the researcher to understand what people should do with the old cultural ways when they become Christians and also how the Christian churches in Myanmar should respond to such a worldview.[75]

Historical research tells us the past events, but ethnographic research tells us both the present and how things turned out that way.[76] The historical and ethnographic mixed method allows the researcher to trace the history of Myanmar Christian missions and how the contemporary Christian theologians got to the present situation. By knowing the past history of Christian missions and how they got here, the churches in Myanmar will know how to prepare for their future mission.

Missiological research requires several different approaches because of the nature of this study – more than one culture and spiritual issue – so it requires multiple viewpoints to know what is happening in the multicultural settings.[77] The selected interviewees stipulated in the research design represent a wide variety of religious groups and ethnicities of Myanmar: Buddhist monks and lay Buddhists from Rakhine, Burmese, and Kayah, and contemporary Christian theologians from evangelical and liberal Christians. The criterion for selecting the interviewees is limited to the accessibility of the persons and their knowledge of the subject matters. Paul Hiebert notes, "cultural differences affect the messengers, but they also affect the message."[78] It is essential to have a variety of cultural backgrounds in the interviews and the researcher's task is to synthesize and analyze various views and make conclusions according to the Scripture. The researcher's responsibility is to interpret all the materials.

---

75. Hiebert, *Anthropological Insights*, 171.
76. Wolcott, *Ethnography*, 1.
77. Elliston, *Missiological Research Design*, xxii.
78. Hiebert, *Anthropological Insights*, 141.

As Bauer and Traina recommend and urge us to approach with a "radical openness to any conclusion required by the biblical evidence," Christian missions in a religiously pluralistic context could lead us to dismiss the true meaning of the biblical missiology.[79] The ultimate reason for using missiological communication approach is that it is solidly grounded on the Scripture and the Trinitarian *missio Dei*. The present research considers the Bible as the primary source and unit of meaning, so as not to depart from the faith expressed in the ecumenical creeds of the Christian church or church confessions as long as we begin with the Scripture.[80] To address the research problem, the present researcher employs Joseph A. Maxwell's concept, "qualitative researchers typically study a relatively small number of individuals or situations and preserve the individuality of each of these in their analyses, rather than collecting data from large samples and aggregating the data across individuals or situations."[81]

---

79. Bauer and Traina, *Inductive Bible Study*, 18.
80. Schulz, "Mission Communication."
81. Bickman and Rog, *Applied Research Methods*, 75.

CHAPTER 2

Scriptural and Confessional Considerations and Literature Review

In this chapter, the researcher will review the literature related to the research title, "A Theology of Mission for Myanmar: Making a Case for the Christian Mission in the Context of Contemporary Theologians' Attempt to Reconcile Nat Worship with Christianity." The researcher has divided the review into several sections: 1. Burmese worldview, (a) God in Myanmar (b) the problem of suffering in the Burmese context, (c) missionaries' attitude toward Nat worship; 2. Missiological reflections on Christ, church, and Nat worship, (a) the suffering of Christ in response to Nat worship, (b) gospel through suffering, (c) the suffering church; and. 3. The role of Nat worship informs life in society, (a) life after death, (b) religious ceremony, (c) sacred and profane in Nat worship.

Burmese Worldview

Before Buddhism became the dominant religion in Myanmar, Nat worship was the primary religion among the indigenous people. When Buddhism was introduced to Myanmar in 300 B.C.,[1] Nat worship was the sole religion practiced among indigenous people for an extended period. The term *"Nat"* is derived from the Pali word to denote worthy of worship. It is the worship of a host spirit that represented local nature gods, the spirit of earth and sky, rain and wind, whirlpool and whirlwind, of mountains, rivers and trees, of the

---

1. Gulati, "Politics of Buddhism."

jungle and in the house.² According to Burmese traditional beliefs, *Nat* can bring various kinds of suffering, fear, illness, harvest failure, and even death.³

Therefore, pleasing the Nat or spirits is absolutely crucial especially if they are not well treated – harvest can fail because they have supernatural power to cause poor soil conditions, insufficient rainfall, and even natural disasters which can damage agricultural life. Simon Pau Khan En, a theologian from Myanmar, suggests that Nat worship demonstrates the same phenomenon as animism⁴ which aligns with what Edward B. Tylor calls "Animism" as the belief in spiritual beings.⁵

In his book, *The Thirty-Seven Nat*, R. C. Temple observes, "In order to understand the daily life and aspirations of the ordinary Burman, it is not sufficient to know that he is by professed religion a Buddhist and to understand what his Buddhism teaches. It is necessary to know also that he is a firm believer in *Nat* and to grasp how the superstitions connected with this faith affect him in his daily life and notions."⁶ Even practitioners can get confused in distinguishing pure Buddhism from the Nat belief system in Myanmar because both systems have numerous functions to which people turn for relief in times of suffering.

Nat worship through exorcism provides an alternative explanation for the cause of suffering when there is no escape from karma. When a person is sick, certain symptoms are thought to be linked with certain spirits. For example, giddiness is the whirlwind spirit; a headache that comes between six and nine o'clock comes from the spirit of the morning star; a demon dwells in waste places, and can be seen rising in the midst; yellow jaundice comes from the spirit of the rainbow.⁷ This belief system is not found in the teachings of the Buddha. However, Nat worship tolerates Burmese Buddhism because it answers social crises through propitiating the *Nat* or spirits. This interaction demonstrates how Nat worship penetrated the fundamental beliefs of Burmese Buddhism. Over time, as Buddhism spread and gained prominence, it incorporated elements of the existing Nat worship practices. This syncretic

---

2. Coupland, *British Empire History*, 13.
3. Spiro, *Burmese Supernaturalism*, 91.
4. En, *Nat Worship*, 177.
5. Tylor, *Primitive Culture*, xii.
6. Temple, *Thirty-Seven Nat*, i.
7. Temple, *Thirty-Seven Nat*, i.

process allowed for the coexistence of Nat worship within the framework of Burmese Buddhism, with the Nat spirits being accommodated and appeased as part of the overall religious belief system. The fusion of these two belief systems reflects the adaptability and inclusive nature of Burmese religious practices, as well as the enduring influence of indigenous traditions within the broader context of Buddhism in Myanmar.

James W. Sire convincingly asserts that everyone has a worldview.[8] Similarly, John Lennox suggests that every one of us needs a worldview to construct our belief system.[9] However, for the Burmese people, it would be the other way around – the belief systems, Nat worship, and Buddhism had shaped the Burmese worldview. The Myanmar government official claimed that "we Burmese are Buddhists" since 1910.[10] It seems as though the religion, Buddhism, came before the worldview of the Burmese people. In other words, worldview does not shape the Burmese belief system, but the belief system shapes their worldview. One of the reasons why the Burmese people's belief system is more important than their worldview is that it became a tool to resist the Western culture and imported religions such as Christianity.[11]

Gooding rightly asserts that worldview is necessary to construct our belief system.[12] Steve Curtis describes the Burmese worldview as a worldview made up of three – animism, Buddhism, and cultural-historical.[13] What exactly is the Burmese worldview? There is no straightforward answer to this question. It is because the Burmese worldview is a merger of two different religions or belief systems, Nat worship and Buddhism. It is best described as a two-tiered system, the belief in both naturalism and supernaturalism. The Burmese worldview agrees with deism – belief in the existence of God on the evidence of reason and nature, but generally it rejects revelation as a source of knowledge.[14] Given that the Burmese worldview intersects with deism

---

8. Sire, *Universe Next Door*, 19.
9. Lennox and Gooding, *Questioning Our Knowledge*, 3.
10. Nyunt, *Mission amidst Pagodas*, 50.
11. Mang, "Christianity and Ethnic Identity," 83.
12. Gooding and Lennox, *Being Truly Human*, 3.
13. Curtis, "Worldviews in Myanmar," 57–83.
14. Sire, *Universe Next Door*, 66.

because it is based on reason and nature, it merges very well with the belief in the supernatural power of Nat worship.[15]

Another difficulty in explaining the Burmese worldview is the lack of an alternative explanation for suffering, which is the underlying rationale for Burmese Buddhists to intermingle with Nat worship. In a strict sense of the term, the alternative explanation for human suffering is the scapegoating of the Burmese people. The interpolation of the scapegoating concept creates the possibility of seeking salvation through the work of someone else which is contradictory to the Buddha's original teaching. This ideology, supernaturalism, leads to the next section, God in Myanmar, because it is fitting to begin the worldview with theism. Also, this ideology provides an overarching approach to understanding God and his relationship to man and the world. Spiro has rightly explained that the Burmese Nat worship is based on supernaturalism and its relation to the traditional Buddhism of the country.[16]

There are other opposite worldviews that Burmese Buddhism holds, for example, the concept of death, hell, heaven, and eternal life. Although, for Burmese Buddhists, there is no eternal life but liberation from Samsara (cycle of rebirth), there is no such thing as death but being *flown away* to *Nibban*, the Nat realm. Buddhism does not accept a vertical form of heaven, earth, and hell because of the belief in the cycle of rebirth in everything. Overall, the amalgamation of the two worldviews system endorses the missiological perspective of the existence of Christian God. The present writer will tease out the biblical worldview for communicating the gospel to the Burmese Nat worship because Christianity is not an amalgamation of two religions, but one founded by Jesus Christ.

John Nisbet affirmed Spiro's statement, "the Burmese Buddhists still worship evil spirits, so in founding the new city he (King Mindon) acted on the advice of his chief astrologer, a pregnant woman was slain one night in order that she might become the guardian spirit of his palace."[17] This is strong proof of Burmese animistic worship in spite of being one of the most devoted Buddhist societies in the world.

---

15. Spiro, *Burmese Supernaturalism*, 23.
16. Spiro, *Burmese Supernaturalism*, 23.
17. Nisbet, *Burma Under British Rule*, 196.

God in Myanmar

This section investigates the Burmese perspective of God concerning their belief systems, Nat worship, and Buddhism. When Christians in Myanmar use the term God, it refers to the eternal God, who is the creator of the universe from the Christian point of view. However, the Burmese Buddhists have denied all ties to the doctrine of God and renounced all speculations about God. It is inconceivable for Burmese Buddhists to see God in a personal form, for there is no personal form of God for the Buddhists.

In some sense, the Burmese Buddhists do not deny the existence of Ultimate Reality, which is very different from the Christian idea of the eternal God. There is a saying in Myanmar, that if you try hard, you can even become a god. However, the researcher aims to elaborate on the God who saves the world.[18] A Western Buddhist, John Makransky, believes there may be possibilities for further discussion that "different religious faiths can relate their adherents to the same ultimate reality through diverse understandings which come to those adherents through socially conditioned forms of their own religious cultures."[19]

The first Western Christian missionary, Adoniram Judson, who translated the Bible into Burmese, initially employed the term *"Phaya"* because there is no other word for God to convey the meaning of the Christian God fully. However, the term *Phaya* suggested a Buddhist pagoda or a Buddha, a monk and a man possessed of supernatural power.[20] The problem was that the term *Phaya* could be the Buddha, monk, and pagoda. So, Judson compared and contrasted the Buddhist doctrine of god, and the Christian doctrine of God.[21]

The Burmese term *Phaya* alone would create confusion for the ordinary people so, in his Bible translation, Judson prefixed a phrase, *"thawarah"* eternal and suffixed *"Thakhin"* Lord to *Phaya* which means the eternal Lord God in his Burmese translation. Judson was aware of the use of the solitary term *Phaya* without the phrase *Thakhin* can be misinterpreted among Burmese society. What would happen if he used only *Phaya*? It can be a monk, a Buddha, and a pagoda. What about if he used *Thakhin* without *Phaya*? The

---

18. Harmon, "Adoniram Judson," 41.
19. Schmidt-Leukel, *Buddhist Attitudes*, 50.
20. Wa and Sowards, *Burmese Baptist Chronicle*, 146.
21. Moe, "Adoniram Judson," 270.

term *Thakhin* is a prefix to national hero and leader. For example, *Thakhin* Aung San, *Thakhin* Mya, and *Thakhin* Tan Tun. The use of the terms, *thawarah Hpaya Thakhin* denotes a Trinitarian God, according to Judson.[22]

For example, Judson's translation of Zephaniah 3:17a "Your Lord God, the eternal God, is in your midst, the mighty God will save you." သင်၏ဘုရားသခင် ထာဝရဘုရားသည် သင့် အလယ်၌ရှိ၍၊ တန်ခိုးကြီး သော ဘုရား သည် သင့် ကို ကယ်တင်တော်မူလိမ့်မည်။[23]

The expression of Christian God in the Burmese Nat context is very important. Therefore, the missionary Judson introduced the Christian God rooted in the concept of a Trinitarian *missio Dei, Htawarah Hpaya Thakhin*. If one uses *Hpaya* to denote Christian God, it would suddenly be assumed that Christians worship a lesser god because even a pagoda, monk, and image of the Buddha is called *Phaya* in the Burmese language. The hypothesis of Judson links three creative ideas: first, he introduced the Christians' God as a Trinitarian Being. Second, he demonstrated that the Christian God is a personal being who wants to relate with human beings. And third, Judson preached that the triune God, the Father, Son, and Holy Spirit is distinctive from other gods.

Problem of Natural Evil in Burmese Context

Before the problem of natural evil in the Burmese context is discussed, the researcher would like to highlight the problem of natural evil in general. John Lennox asks, "If there is a God in heaven who is all-powerful, all-wise, and all-loving, and is supposed to care for justice, why does he allow such evil to continue?"[24] Why does he not prevent innocent people from such moral evil and suppress those who perpetrate it, and put an end to evil?

It seems as though God does not protect innocent people, particularly from brutality. If so, a common reaction is to abandon all faith in God and decide that atheism must be true. However, the opposite is true. It is very challenging to know what is morally evil or good without the existence of a standard by which something is judged. The logical conclusion is that if there is not any moral standard of good, then the problem of moral evil is dissolved

---

22. Bailey, *Adoniram Judson*, 61.
23. *Holy Bible in Burmese*, 947.
24. Gooding and Lennox, *Suffering Life's Pain*, 45.

because there is no moral standard to judge whether something is good or evil.[25] Even if moral standards are made by sinful human beings, good morals cannot be produced. Although atheism seems at first to solve the problem, as God seems to be silent in the face of evil, it proves to make the problem worse because atheism does not provide any standard to measure what is good and evil. John Lennox asserts, "some atheists deny that there is any such thing as moral good and evil."[26] To put it in another way, the atheist's ground ceases to be meaningful and is incoherent with the logical conclusion. In theism, God is the authority behind good and evil, and he will be the final judgment.

The history of Myanmar's Christian mission went through several political transitions such as monarchy, colonialism, parliamentary, anocracy-democracy, socialist regime, and currently, military dictatorship. In 1962, General Ni Win turned Myanmar into one of the poorest countries in the world. His successor, Than Shwe, was a much crueler leader who led the country further into destruction through human rights violations and economic exploitation. Finally, General Min Aung Hlaing led the military coup on 1 February 2021, and seized the democratically elected leaders, President Win Myint, and the State Counsellor of Myanmar, Aung San Suu Kyi.

On 23 July 2022, the military brutally executed four pro-democracy activists. They were hanged by the junta. According to the *Irrawaddy News*, the junta regime set another 41 to be executed as the political prisoners with yellow uniforms have been moved to a different cell in preparation for the execution.[27] History tells us that the rulers of Myanmar were notorious murderers. For example, King Bagyidaw murdered two of his uncles and two hundred other officials. Pagan Min's grandson put six thousand Burmese to death for the purpose of profit.[28]

The problem of suffering in Myanmar is related to all spheres of life, including socioeconomic and religiopolitical settings. One can look at the suffering of Myanmar from various perspectives because it is social and political in nature, and historical in a sense as well as spiritual in content. In the strict sense of the term, suffering is so real and at the same time complex in

---

25. Gooding and Lennox, *Suffering Life's Pain*, 49.
26. Gooding and Lennox, *Suffering Life's Pain*, 49.
27. *The Irrawaddy News*, English Edition, 28 July, 2022.
28. Geiseman, *Men and Missions*, 9.

the context of Myanmar. The root causes of suffering are a political crisis, civil war, and human rights violations in all dimensions of life.

Interestingly, Myanmar was one of the first countries that enthusiastically endorsed the Universal Declaration of Human Rights (UDHR) adopted in 1948.[29] Then, however, the military regime overturned the endorsement of human rights by removing religious rights that deprived the fundamental human rights of ethnic minorities. Today, however, they have applied a very different method saying that the Universal Declaration of Human Rights is based on the Western concepts of government. Moreover, it is a tool for Western cultural imperialism imposed on us that ignores the distinctive cultural values of the Burmese people.[30]

U Nu, the former prime minister, adopted the notion of one religion, one nation, and one language. The promulgation of Buddhism as the state religion and cultural assimilation into the predominant group of Myanmar Buddhists have become the biggest problem for the other religions, Christianity and Islam. The Anglican missionaries in Myanmar saw education as an essential part of mission since their inception in 1877. The formal education taught by Christian missionaries included Bible studies and thus attracted many to convert to Christianity.[31] Following the nationalization of school, religion, and the economy, a government official alleges a straightforward policy of Burmanization or Myanmarization. The Burmese Bible, translated by Adoniram Judson in the 1820s, never received permission to be printed in Myanmar. The promulgation of Buddhism as a state religion is a means of national integration and religious assimilation; that is another way for religious persecution.

The problem of suffering has indeed been ingrained in the life of the Burmese people from time immemorial. Therefore, alleviating social injustice is the best solution to the protracted political conflict. The Buddha taught human beings to observe the tenets or the four noble truths and the eightfold path to avoid all kinds of suffering.[32] In the Christian point of view, however, the problem of suffering is inherited from Adam that affects all races, as

---

29. In 1948, the UN had fifty-six member countries; forty-eight countries voted for the Universal Declaration of Human Rights.

30. Sakhong, *In Defense of Identity*, 35.

31. Doe, *Discipling the Church*, 19.

32. Dhammananda, *What Buddhists Believe*, 83.

stated in Romans 3:10, "there is none righteous, no, not one," and Romans 3:23, "For all have sinned and fall short of the glory of God." Therefore, the problem of natural evil, which affects all human beings cannot be solved by natural means. According to Buddhism, man is not sinful by nature; therefore, everyone is a good person who has within himself a vast store of good and evil habits.[33]

The teaching of the Buddha is correlational to the concept of the Western enlightenment that posits everything is begun from within a person, and he is the maker of his own destiny. George Wald, Bertrand Russell, and many other modern thinkers affirmed that the final value of a man is the biological continuity of the human race.[34] Schaeffer writes, "now having traveled from the pride of man in the High Renaissance and the Enlightenment down to the present despair, we can understand where modern people are. They have no place for a personal God. But, equally they have no place for man as man, or for love, or for freedom, or significance. It brings a cruel problem."[35]

Missionaries and Contemporary Theologians' Attitudes Toward Nat Worship

Missionaries are to live and work in a world made up of different people, languages, and cultures where they go in service. A common term that often appears is the people's culture and religion.[36] Throughout the history of Christian missionary endeavor, some missionaries saw their religio-culture as paganism and worshiped false gods. They labeled the animistic practice as savage, barbaric, and uncivilized.[37] Others accepted them without a critical analyzation of the culture and religion of the people and syncretized the indigenous religious system with Christianity.

This section outlines the attitudes of some missionaries and contemporary Myanmar theologians toward the Burmese Nat-Buddhists. The first Western missionaries to Myanmar were two Italian Catholic priests in A.D. 1720, and they established a few local churches in A.D.1740.[38] They were followed by

---

33. Dhammananda, *What Buddhists Believe*, 99.
34. Schaeffer, *How Should We?*, 166.
35. Schaeffer, *How Should We?*, 166.
36. Reed, *Preparing Missionaries*, 119.
37. Nehrbass, *Christianity and Animism*, xi.
38. Trager, *Burma through Alien Eyes*, 9.

another Catholic missionary, Fr. Vinentious Sangermano in July 1783, who established the church of St. John, which became St. John School. He was highly esteemed by the native people simply because his efforts enabled poor rural communities to benefit from primary education.[39] It was quite an honor that the ruler of the country visited the church while Fr. Sangermano was the head of the institution. It got public interest as many local people could access primary education. In 1834, the Burmese official requested Mr. Bennet who had worked for the mission press in Moulmein in Myanmar, to start a government English school, and he did it.[40]

Everything changed when the first American Baptist missionary, Adoniram Judson, came to Myanmar on 13 July 1813. Judson treated Burmese Nat worship as an atheistic and false religious practice.[41] However, Judson accepted the Burmese Buddhist terms as sacred language in his mission communication. As a result of his attitude toward Burmese Nat worship and Buddhists in Myanmar, Judson indescribably suffered seventeen months in the most horrible jails for the sake of Christ in Myanmar.[42] The Catholic foreign missionaries generously established churches and schools for the benefit of the native people, and therefore were not subject to any persecution. In contrast, the American Baptist missionary Judson was jailed three times during his missionary work in Myanmar. He cried out, "In spite of sorrow, loss, and pain, our course be onward still; we sow on Burma's barren plain, we reap on Zion's hill."[43] This was not the end, it was the beginning as the Judsons had started their very own Baptist church with ten members despite facing the possibility of persecution and death by the Burmese government.

Another couple, Arthur and Laura Carson, were the first American missionaries to the Chin people in northwestern Myanmar. They encouraged people to abandon their way of life and adhere to the Christian way. Arthur and Laura's attitude toward traditional practice was both negative and positive. They were negative toward the primal religious practice as it mingled with spirit worship. However, they were positive toward constructing schools,

---

39. Sangermano, *Description of Burmese Empire*, 116.
40. Sangermano, *Description of Burmese Empire*, 116.
41. Dingrin, "Conflicting Legacy," 485–97.
42. Mathieson, *Judson of Burma*, 84.
43. Judson wrote this phrase after his second child passed away.

medical work, and agriculture. The missionaries tried not only to educate and Christianize but also to provide the means by which the native people would be able to support a higher civilization.[44] Joseph Herbert Cope, another American missionary to the Chin people, once said, "The only hope of getting Christianity firmly established in these hills is to smash the existing social structure of the Chin life."[45]

It cannot be merely considered that Judson's attitude toward Burmese Nat worship was negative, as he embraced the Burmese Pali terms as indispensable for his Bible translation work and evangelism. Judson acknowledged the importance of using the Burmese language and culture in constructing a theology of mission. For example, Judson used the Burmese terms, *thavarah phaya* – eternal God – to refer to Christian God in his Burmese Bible translation. For the sake of the gospel, Judson changed his attitude toward the Burmese people and gave up all as a translator between the British and Burmese. After Judson learned the Burmese language, the British colonists came to the country, and he was hired as a translator with a reasonable fee. However, he gave up after he realized it was not appropriate to compromise the mission of God with social services.

There have been two different attitudes between Catholic and Baptist missionaries toward the Burmese Nat worship. The former embraced Nat worship, and the latter treated it as paganism and as anti-Christian. On the one hand, the Baptist missionaries accepted Burmese and Pali as a sacred language for mission communication. On the other, the Catholic missionaries did not use the language for mission communication among the Burmese society. Therefore, it is appropriate to highlight Apostle Paul's attitude toward the Corinthians as a missionary. It could be said that Paul's attitude toward the Corinthians was similar to those of the Baptist missionaries in Myanmar because Paul proclaimed that there is only one God and Lord, and all other gods are false.[46] The cities in which Paul preached the gospel were home to pagan worship.[47] Nat worship and Buddhism had been embedded in the land for over two thousand years before Judson brought the gospel to Myanmar.

---

44. Bawihrin, "Impact of Missionary Christianity," 45.
45. 157th Confidential File, 1936–37, of Deputy Commissioner Office, Falam, folio 59.
46. Nissen, *New Testament and Mission*, 99.
47. Allen, *Missionary Methods*, 27.

In a heathen land like Myanmar, it was a bold decision to preach constantly the supremacy of Christ over all indigenous belief systems and that it takes a real Savior to deliver them from their dark world.[48]

The missionary should respect the culture of the people in the mission field because God is the author of human culture, and missionaries are called to transform it by proclaiming the gospel of Christ. Paul G. Hiebert, a missiologist and anthropologist, succinctly divided into three categories the ways in which Christian missionaries should respond to a particular culture. These are material culture, expressive culture, and ritual culture. Paul Hiebert observes that in material culture, people make objects for entertainment or cure and then these become cultural practices. For example, the Burmese purportedly cure the sick by burying small images of the sick people in tiny coffins as protective charms. Expressive culture is the expression of people's feelings through music in times of joy or sorrow. The most challenging situation for Christian missionaries is the ritual culture in a new cultural setting.[49]

The objects, music or song, and ritual for events such as birthday, marriage, and death need to be critically analyzed according to the biblical point of view. For instance, the Burmese practice of burying small images of sick people to cure them is not biblical but idolatry. The music they play during funeral ceremonies and birthday events is not biblical. In Myanmar, the local form of Theravada Buddhism is attached to the worship of local spirits, called Nat worship. Devotees observe the ceremony and pray to invoke the spirits to obtain health and wealth. The ceremony includes the scents of flowers, food, and perfume followed by the sound of the music accompanying the spirit possession dances.

During the ceremony, the dancers or *nat kadaw*[50] act as a spirit medium, calling up the spirits in a precise order and offering their bodies as a vessel for the Nat. In 2004, the writer witnessed a Burmese family which followed Nat worship next to his house in Yangon, holding a ritual ceremony where the guest dancer, *nat kadaw*, bit raw chicken as a result of spirit possession. This kind of ceremony is called "*nat pwe*," meaning the inherent ambivalent

---

48. Allen, *Missionary Methods*, 28.

49. Hiebert, *Anthropological Insights*, 171–77.

50. Nat Kadaw is a Burmese term to denote wife of nat. In the strict sense of the term, it means "women who possess(ed) spirits."

spirits normally held in the private home of a devotee. A temporary bamboo pavilion is erected for this occasion. Usually, the sacred images of the spirits believed to be alive, are surrounded by various offerings such as flowers, cash, and food.

The time is overdue for Myanmar Christians to address Burmese Nat worship according to the Scripture adequately. If new philosophical ideas and technological advances can lead to cultural change, the gospel's power can change the culture. Cultural change means creating new ideas, and while it does not mean just adopting innovation one after another, it does mean producing the capacity for reculturing that involves hard work.[51] When confronting idolatry and spirit worship in mission fields, no one comes close to the missionary, apostle Paul. In the process of preaching the gospel, Paul frequently uses different verbs; he warns, admonishes, instructs, teaches, and explains to the people concerning wrong beliefs and practices. The biblical reasons worthy of quoting Paul's letter are that he was a missionary, evangelist, pastor, and teacher, and most importantly, he wrote more than half of the New Testament.[52] For example, Paul preached to the people of Lystra and proclaimed the true God according to Acts 14:15b, "we are bringing to you good news, telling you to turn from these worthless things to the living God." His statement clearly shows that those who worship the true God must turn away from the traditional gods. Moreover, the scriptural passage indicates that they did not properly distinguish between gods and human beings as Acts 14:11 says, "the gods have come down to us in human form. Barnabas, they called Zeus, and Paul, they called Hermes because he was the chief speaker."

The apostle Paul commanded his audience in Lystra that the deities they worshiped were worthless and that the people needed to turn away from their idols. In the same way, Myanmar Christians should encourage new converts and even non-Christians to turn away from Nat worship. According to Paul's letters, the action of turning away from the traditional deities means ending the practice of bowing before the image of a deity. Turning away also meant refraining from worshiping and offering sacrifices. The apostle Paul did not simply stop them from worshiping national deities, he declared that he brought the good news that it is possible to worship the living God (Acts

---

51. Fullan, *Leading in a Culture*, 44.
52. Schnabel, *Paul the Missionary*, 144.

14:15). In other words, he preached the supremacy of Christ over against the local deities of the heathen people.[53] So also, Christian missionaries today need to preach the same Christ against local deities.

Given the latent form of Nat worship and its ritual activities in the context of Myanmar, the situation during the time of Paul in Lystra and Corinth had similar practices to that of the Burmese Nat worship. In sharp contrast to the apostle Paul, a Myanmar theologian, Simon Pau Khan En, endorses Nat worship as a source of theology in Myanmar. En provides three elements which he thinks would be the source of a theology of mission in Myanmar: the worldview of Burmese Nat worship, the concept of a supreme being, and the concept of ecology. This worldview helps us see human's relationship with God, where the concept of supreme being serves as a *praeparatio evangelica*, and the ecological view provides us that every object and landscape is inhabited by Nat, and it teaches Christians about the deep sense of stewardship.[54] The following section will delve deep into the missionary's attitude toward Nat worship through a reflection of Christ and his church. In contrast to that of En's concept, Terry Mark states that mission means the expansion of Christianity among non-Christians.[55]

Missiological Reflections on Christ, Church, and Nat Worship

There are two common missiological approaches to proclaiming the gospel of Christ. The first general approach starts with the Scripture and then proceeds to the context and the second approach starts with the context and then proceeds to the Scripture. The question lies at the heart of the biblical missiological reflections as to where Christians start. There are two pressing reasons: *expressionist semiotic* was invented by Augustine; the latter is the *efficacious external means of grace* developed by Philip Cary. The former has to do with the inner self as the divine intellectual, whereby man rejecting material things and purifying his soul can lift it to communion with God.

---

53. Schnabel, *Paul the Missionary*, 165.
54. En, "Nat Worship: A Paradigm," 47–49.
55. Terry, *Missiology: An Introduction*, 4.

Augustine, adopting from Platonian philosophy, views the inner soul as an invisible spiritual reality that becomes a higher spiritual reality.[56] In other words, Augustinian concepts start with the human context and proceed to God. The latter concept, *efficacious external means of grace*, means Christians allow the *external* word of God to be revealed to us so that one starts with the word "Logos" and then proceeds to the human context. The human inner self has no sufficient capacity to grasp God, who is beyond description. Hence, Christians must start with the scriptural authority to understand God's created things. Given the two radical concepts above, authentic Christians should be able to make a sharp distinction between the two approaches by now.

The greatest single verse in the New Testament might be John 1:14 which says, "So the Word of God became a person, and took up his abode in our being, full of grace and truth; and we looked with our own eyes upon his glory, glory like the glory which an only son receives from his father." There was an Ephesian philosopher called Heraclitus whose basic idea was constructing everything on Logos. He discovered that everything was in a state of flux. In other words, everything changes from day to day and from moment to moment.

He finally acknowledged that everything changing is controlled and ordered by the Logos, the word, the reason of God. For him, "the Logos was the principle of the order under which the universe continued to exist."[57] Heraclitus held that not only was Logos the principle of the existence of the physical world but was also a pattern in the world of events. For him, everything is changing and moving according to the purpose of the Logos. His discovery perfectly fits John 1:1 and 14.

Constructing a missiological approach to the Burmese Nat worship from the standpoint of the Logos will contrast with that of the contemporary liberal theologians in Myanmar. They proceed from Nat worship to the Logos. Logos is the power that made the world, the power that keeps the order of things in the world, and the power by which humans think and know. The Logos is the principle controlling everything, including the Burmese Nat worship. The Logos, word of God, is the foundation of the world. There was a man called Philo of Alexandria, born in 25 B.C. William Barclay noted that no

---

56. Cary, *Outward Signs*, 182.
57. Schulz, "Word Became Flesh," 4.

one knew the Jewish scripture as Philo knew; no Jew ever knew the greatness of Greek thought as he knew it. Philo too knew and used the idea of Logos, the word, and held that the Logos was the oldest thing in the world and the instrument through which God had made the world. He added that the Logos was the thought of God.[58]

The invention of the *zayat* for the locus of witnessing Christ amidst pagodas is quite interesting. Judson proceeded from the Logos to the context as he knew that the Logos is the Word that gave birth to *ecclesia*, the church. Instead of identifying the *ecclesia* with Nat worship, Judson identified *ecclesia* with the *zayat* to identify Christ with the church.

In contrast, Myanmar liberal theologians suggest that the traditional concept of conversion does not necessarily identify with Christianity and the church.[59] The *zayat* serves a different purpose from the Buddhist perspective. In a tropical season in Myanmar, the *zayat* provides shelter and rest for travelers and a place to gather, talk, and share local news. It would have been easier for Judson to approach Buddhist-Nat worship if he had identified *ecclesia*, the church, with pagodas.

There are four specific reasons why Judson's missiological approach is unique. First, Judson encountered extreme difficulties in communicating the gospel to Burmese Buddhist-Nat worshipers. Second, his missiological approach was person-to-person evangelism in a round-table model. Third, the influence of the Western philosophy of individualism still affected his missiological approach. Fourth, Judson's mission strategy seemed to focus more on receiving visitors in his home than visiting their home. He did not win any converts within the first five years, but he learned the importance of utilizing the *zayat* and as a result, he won U Naw on April 30, 1819.[60]

Situating the church of Christ into a Burmese Nat context must take four serious aspects. First, the newly planted church must be coherent with the primary understanding of the New Testament church. Second, the church is established in such a way that both the church and the world encounter each other. Third, the church in the world must have the capacity to handle the total life of the church by providing the word of God to every member

---

58. Schulz, "Word Became Flesh," 5.
59. En, "Quest for Authentic Myanmar," 64.
60. Mathieson, *Judson of Burma*, 90.

and being the role model of the community. There is a critical distinction between the church and the world. It maintains a critical distinction between the two, yet one cannot exist without the other. Fourth, situating the church in a Nat worship context is rooted in the history of the church (Matt 16:18).

If the church that is built on the Rock, Jesus Christ, is identified with local gods or national deities, it is no longer the church. Every Christian easily answers a simple question, "What is church?" A German professor Johannes Reimer suggests, "in reality, however, the question is much more complicated as the amount of literature on the nature of the church proves. We are well advised to go back to the New Testament for an adequate answer."[61] Reimer quotes, "Jesus replied to Simon son of Jonah that you are Peter, and on this rock, I will build my church" as the adequate answer to what is church in the world.[62]

The perspective of the church in the world needs to be crystal clear. As Christ is the head of the church, the mission of the church should flow from the mission of Christ, which is rooted in a triune God. This is to denote that the mission of the church is moving away from a human prerogative and activity to a divine one. Therefore, *missio ecclesiae* comes alone from the *missio Dei*. Unfortunately, many theologians failed to link the *missio ecclesiae* to the *missio Dei* to define the mission of the church in the world. The problem lies in the relationship between the church and the world.[63] Therefore, how one conceives the *missio ecclesiae* is vital in relating to the world. For example, a Dutch missiologist, J. C. Hoekendijk, effectively marginalized the role of the church in the *missio Dei* and placed the world at the center of God's activity. In other words, the church is called to follow the instruction of the world.[64]

The polemic against the biblical meaning of the church is largely due to defining mission in terms of social services. A biblical church would negate itself if it denied the obligation to preach the gospel to the heathen. Without an understanding of the divine nature of the church, the fellowship of believers is unstable and aimless. If a missionary does not know the church and is not able to develop antitheses of the doctrine, he will never bring forth

---

61. Reimer, *Missio Politica*, chapter 5.
62. Reimer, chapter 5.
63. Ott, ed., *Mission of Church*, xiv.
64. Ott, *Mission of Church*, xv.

the mission of the church correctly. He would have to teach his own gospel, which is not from the Scripture.[65]

If En's suggestion in constructing a theology of mission based on the three factors, "the Burmese worldview, belief in a supreme being, and ecological concept" is to be employed for the Burmese Nat worship context, then one loses sight in biblical missiology, because it starts with human context. As Gadamer put it, "The logos is the stream that flows from this thought and sounds out through the mouth."[66] The Logos, the word of God, is the accurate starting point to approach paganism.

The apostle Paul is best known for addressing pagan gods in his epistles. He succinctly differentiates between the one true God and man-made idolatry in Lystra in Acts 14:8–18, and between deities and the unknown god at Athens in Acts 17:23. Paul forbid Christians to participate in the sacrificial offering in pagan temples at Corinth (1 Cor 8:1–11), and to Diana, goddess for Ephesians (Acts 19:28) (NKJV).

The account in Acts 19:27–28 has a context similar to that of the Burmese Nat worship in Myanmar. The similarity of the Acts context is that Paul preached the gospel in Ephesus, a pagan context similar to that of Myanmar. As the ultimate goal of Nat worship is to please the evil spirits to bring fortunes, wealth, healing, and so on, the worship of Diana for Ephesians also was to bring prosperity. There are two specific ways Ephesians benefited from Diana the goddess, so they thought.

First, the local silversmith business was one of their main resources because persons who came from afar to worship the goddess at the temple of Ephesus bought silver shrines.[67] One of the reasons for Paul's imprisonment at Ephesus was his successful gospel ministry that, after conversion to Christianity people stopped buying silver shrines and idols from the silversmiths which significantly damaged their local business.[68] Therefore, the Ephesians accused Paul of damaging the local silversmith market as they no longer sold at their normal pace. Acts 19:24 says, "A silversmith named Demetrius, who made silver shrines of Artemis, brought in a lot of business

---

65. Petri, *Mission and Church*.
66. Gadamer, *Truth and Method*, 408.
67. Henry and Scott, *Matthew Henry's Concise Commentary*.
68. Elwell and Yarbrough, *Encountering New Testament*, 244.

for the craftsmen there." When many who believed Paul's preaching confessed and denounced their previous practices, the silversmith assumed Paul brainwashed the Ephesians.

By his proclamation of Christian messages, the people of Ephesus felt that Paul rebelled against their goddess, and she was robbed of her majesty because, at one point, he said human-made images are not gods.[69] Visitors to the Ephesian temple purchased Diana's statue and a shrine made of silver as memorials of their visit and placed them in houses as a charm.

Second, the image of Diana was in the form of an imposing huntress and a many-breasted female, in the form of an idol that was believed to have fallen from heaven (Acts 19:35). The image of Diana was not only sold out to individuals but also set up for worship in other cities. The worshipers believed that the many-breasted female image of Diana represented an ancient goddess of fertility. The statue of Diana, built about 550 B. C. of pure white marble, was four hundred twenty-five feet long by two hundred twenty broad. It was one of the world's wonders and believed to bring prosperity to those who propitiated it.[70] Demetrius continuously said in Acts 19:27 that not only the local economy was in danger of disrepute but also the great goddess was being disdained on the earth. As a result of mass conversion to Christianity, the local authority complained that the temples of the gods and goddess were being forsaken. However, the people reportedly made animal sacrificial offerings again after the arrest of many Christians.[71]

Syncretism is not new today, but it was perhaps the most prevalent characteristic of religion in the Hellenistic age. A New Testament scholar, Ben Witherington III, explains from Acts 15 that there was an agreement that the Gentile converts did not need to be circumcised but did need to avoid idolatry and immorality that transpired in pagan temples. "They are not to attend idol feasts in idol temples."[72] Acts 15:20 speaks of avoiding the pollution of idols and eating idol meat in a pagan temple. It is clear from the book of Acts that the Gentile convert should not syncretize with pagan worship. In the same way, the Burmese converts should not syncretize and they should turn away

---

69. Gundry, *Commentary on New Testament*, 540.
70. Jamieson, Fausset, and Brown, *Commentary*, 1997.
71. Keener, *IVP Bible Background*, 385.
72. Witherington, *New Testament History*, 198.

from Nat worship to the one true God. It is essential to look at what other Scripture passages say about syncretism and idolatry.

The original word for "idol" is derived from *Eidolon* (εἴδωλον) and primarily denotes an idealized person or thing or phantom or likeness, and an appearance. Paul wrote that when the Corinthians were pagans, they were led astray by man-made idols, images representing false gods (1 Cor 12:2).[73] The corresponding Hebrew word for idol conveys vanity, for instance, Jeremiah 14:22 says, "Do any of the worthless idols of the nations bring rain? Do the skies themselves send down showers?" (NIV). So, what represented a deity to the Gentiles was a vain thing for Paul:

> Men, why are you doing these things? We also are men, of like nature with you, and we bring you good news, that you should turn from these vain things to a living God, who made the heaven and the earth and the sea and all that is in them (Acts 14:15).

Paul constantly appeals to the Gentiles to "turn from idolatry to serve a living and true God" (Rom 1:18–32; 1 Thess 1:9). The conversion from idols did not merely limit their worship of idols but included a broader sense of allegiance to anything false. The missiological meaning of conversion from idols to the one true God and the goal of Paul's preaching was a total transformation.[74] If Christians in Myanmar want a total transformation from the bondage of Nat worship – spirit worship – to the one true God, one must avoid the practice of Nat worship.

The Suffering of Christ in Response to Nat Worship

There are two solid responses to Nat worship from the suffering of Christ. First, the suffering of Christ was a *sine qua non* for the redemption of the world. Second, the suffering of Christ brought the glorification of God. However, though Christians have pointed to the cross as a solution for suffering, it is an inevitable question for the Burmese people because, for them, the tragic, frightening, and brutal death of Jesus was only due to his own sin. Therefore, this section makes sense of the reality that Christ died for all

---

73. Vine, *Expository Dictionary*, 573.
74. Senior and Stuhlmueller, *Biblical Foundations*, 186.

human beings. The researcher thinks that making sense of *Christ died for us* is the most challenging task in the world.

First, the primary purpose of the suffering of Christ is to redeem man back from his enemy, Satan. That is possible only by the Son of God becoming a human being. Jeff B. Pool called this "the divine suffering of Christ and the divine wound of God: God suffers because of human fault or sin."[75] The suffering of Christ is necessary for fulfilling the Scripture. The scriptural necessity of the suffering Christ is foretold so that the other predictions of his redemption, resurrection, second coming, and glorification will also be fulfilled.[76] Acknowledging that Jesus is fully human and God along with the perspective of suffering can be difficult to understand. As we acknowledged that Jesus is fully man and fully God, each nature remains distinct and separate from the other. But Jesus is one person within whom the two natures are united, but not compromised.

Christians have long debated whether God can suffer like a human being. "Tertullian, in his *Against Praxeas*, refuted the idea of Patripassianism by asserting that God the Father cannot suffer with the Son on the cross."[77] However, there have been theologians, including Luther, Kitamori, and Moltmann, who strongly advocate the concept that God can suffer for the sake of sinful human nature. Since this section is more about the suffering of Christ than the theological debate between the passibility and impassibility of God, the writer focuses more on the suffering of Christ for his redemptive work in the context of Burmese Nat worship. Among the three great theologians mentioned above, it is worthy of singling out Luther and Kitamori to explore the idea of God's pain and the suffering of Christ, which brings the good news to the sinners.

Luther was probably one of the first theologians to address the concept of the pain of God. For Luther, sin is the enemy of a holy and righteous God, and therefore it insults and wounds God. He must redeem man from the enemy. As a result, though he is not a God of wrath but love and grace, he responds to sinners with wrath. Luther indicates the wrath of God is not an expression of his essence but the undeniable relational entity existing between

---

75. Pool, *God's Wounds*.
76. Wilson, *Saving Cross*, 132.
77. Park, *Wounded Heart*, 111.

God and sinners.[78] Luther views the suffering of Christ as dealing with real sin, not an imaginary sin. Luther purposefully mentioned an imaginary sin as a reaction to what Augustine said, "Sin is something which should never be forgiven, but imaginary sin is already something that can be forgiven."[79]

Sin is not merely imaginary and invisible, but it is real and pervasive. The love of God toward humans conquered his wrath and dissolved sin through the redemptive work of his Son. The pain of God explains the pain we feel when a loved one dies. God exposes his love by using a dreadful reality of man's pain as a testimony to his own pain. The suffering of Jesus on the cross is an active resistance to evil. It is the moment of the apparent loss of his enemy that marks the turning point that assures final victory.[80] Some theologians are more concerned about the profound significance of other aspects of Jesus's death in relation to social evil, but this research is more about the redemptive work of Jesus for eternal liberation from spiritual death than temporary social evil and suffering.

In contrast to Christianity, the Burmese believe that Nat causes suffering to a human being, whereas humans cause suffering to Jesus Christ. In other words, God takes the initiative to take away the suffering through his own divine suffering, whereas the Nat worshipers take responsibility to take away the suffering through appropriate propitiation. Wrath is not the expression of the essence of the Christian God but the true expression of the Burmese Nat because Nat imposes harm, misfortune, illness, and even death on whom they are displeased.

God imposes grace and love on whom he pleases because they cannot please God through their own effort. The condition of Burmese Nat depends on the treatment of human beings, whereas God has unconditional love and grace that does not depend on human good work. In attempting to comprehend the pain and suffering of human beings, John Lennox pointed out two issues: First, he says, "there is something wrong with human nature. The consistent witness of so much evil in human nature. Second, the cause is that man early on used his God-given free will to disgrace his Creator over

---

78. Park, *Wounded Heart*, 114.
79. Kitamori, *Theology*, 35.
80. Heim, *Saved from Sacrifice*, 5–6.

what constitutes life and death, to transgress the parameters God had set on human life, to disobey his word."[81]

Gooding and Lennox proved that the concept of suffering in Nat worship is inconsistent because suffering is the consequence of human disobedience to God, it does not necessarily originate from Nat, but God designed it. In other words, God has the final authority to impose suffering on anyone, including the Nat. If Christians in Myanmar are going to seriously communicate with the Burmese Nat worship, missionaries, pastors, and evangelists need to address the mystery of suffering.

According to Kitamori, the mystery of Christ's suffering is the hidden truth that one must have clear eyes through God's love because our natural eyes cannot see it.[82] For him, the gospel is bound up with the suffering of Christ because God must sentence sinners to death as sinful human nature is against his character and being. Luther sees this fighting with God at Golgotha. It does not mean the fighting of two different gods, but the same God causes his pain in order to heal our wounds. In other words, God suffers wounds, himself receiving his wrath through the death of his Son. Kitamori says, "the historical Jesus and the pain of God cannot be separated." One cannot think of the gospel without God's love toward sinners. This means that the love of God causes suffering and produces the Gospel.[83] Kitamori views the gospel of Christ springing forth from the pain of God.

Right from the beginning, God took the initiative to remove people's sins and to suffer so that death shall not overcome and retain his creature, humankind. After his death from the crucifixion on the cross, Jesus was resurrected from death, and he did not leave his physical body to decay in the grave. The Jews condemned Jesus and delivered him to crucifixion, but God raised him up (Acts 2:23–24). At his second coming, the dead shall be raised, and those still living shall be transformed; all shall have bodies like Christ's glorified body; immortal and incorruptible (1 Cor 15:50–58; Phil 3:20–21). God's glory is decreed from all eternity to reveal the greatness of the glory of his love and grace for his creature. That is possible through the suffering of Jesus Christ,

---

81. Gooding and Lennox, *Suffering Life's Pain*, 150.
82. Kitamori, *Theology*, 19.
83. Kitamori, *Theology*, 20.

the Son of God, who came in the flesh to die and save the undeserving sinners. That is the supreme manifestation of the greatness and the glory of God.

Burmese Nat worshipers perceived that if God is the creator of the universe, then he is responsible for suffering as it is part of this creation. In one sense, it is true that God is accountable for suffering because he has the power to impose and remove suffering any time he wants. Therefore, suffering is an inevitable theme in Christianity, Burmese Nat worship, and Buddhism. For Christianity, to borrow Sunquist's words, "Jesus is the suffering love of God for the world."[84] For Nat worship, suffering occurs when a person infuriates Nat or spirits with an inappropriate offering that displeases Nat. It brings twofold meanings of suffering. According to Christianity, God's wrath on human beings caused pain and suffering on him, whereas Nat's wrath on human beings caused them to suffer as human beings. For Christianity, human suffering is the consequence of disgrace to their creator, and the suffering of Christ is for his own glory and the instrument by which God justified sinners.

In the case of human suffering of Nat worshipers, sorcerers, diviners, and shamans are consulted to find the paraphernalia to offer appropriate rituals. The role of the diviner is to chant his prayer to restore a healthy relationship with the Nat. If Nat is satisfied with the propitiation, the sick person will improve, and the misfortune will be elevated. If not, the sacrificial animal has to be increased to a bigger animal until Nat is satisfied.

Second, the ultimate reason for divine suffering is to display the power and glory of the grace of God. The wrath of God upon human beings is caused by human disobedience. However, God, full of grace and love, has no hesitation in sharing human nature to suffer so his wrath would be propitiated and therefore God and human beings reconciled. As far as Burmese Nat worship is concerned, the ultimate goal of propitiation is to avoid and alleviate human suffering from illness, poverty, conflict, and misfortune with the help of Nat or spirits. Because until now, Buddhist karma has no alternative solution for human suffering. Hence, Nat worship becomes a *sine qua non* for a healthy society.

The suffering of Christ on the cross and his resurrection from death become a legitimate counteraction and an antidote to human suffering, mainly for their spiritual life. Spiro once cited an incident in which the Burmese Nat

---

84. Sunquist, *Understanding Christian Mission*, 199.

worship technique failed to perform miracles. It reads, "This case involved a philandering husband and his wife's attempt to break up his latest affair. For a fee of Kyat 30 ($6.00), the witch-master coerced some demonic spirits to cause the husband and his mistress to quarrel during coitus. The violence of their quarrel led to their arrest and jailing."[85] Employing the Burmese Nat principles to escape from suffering brought shame and bewilderment. However, the theology of glory came from the cross of Christ, which radiates God's love to the world. In the Burmese Nat context, when the witch-masters failed to perform miracles, shame and loss came upon the witch and the followers. But God never failed to glorify Jesus.

Gospel through Suffering

This section focuses on the twofold meanings of the gospel as a response to Burmese Nat worship. First, the power of the gospel, and second, the grace of the gospel.[86] What is the gospel? The term *gospel* goes back to the Old English word *godspel* meaning "good tidings."[87] It is mentioned over 90 times in the Bible. Broadly speaking, the gospel is the mega narrative of God's plan to reconcile humanity to himself.[88] That is why Paul described his primary missionary goal as preaching the gospel.[89]

First, the power of the gospel overcomes sin and death through the resurrection of the Son of God. Apostle Paul called this the pure gospel, which remitted sins through the power of the gospel.[90] Not only did the gospel overcome death, but also it overthrew and destroyed the devil and his kingdom. The power of the gospel lies in the suffering of Christ, where the Burmese Buddhists and Nat worship cannot see it as a ransom for many. Missiologically, Buddhism and Nat worship take an anti-Christian stance. For example, Burmese Buddhism is an atheistic system that rejects the existence of a personal God, and Nat worship is a true expression of that atheism. It is pagan in nature by worshiping evil spirits. Although there is power in the gospel, which springs from the cross of Christ, the Burmese think that such

---

85. Spiro, *Burmese Supernaturalism*, 25.
86. Newbigin, *Gospel*, 175.
87. Schnabel, *Paul the Missionary*, 210.
88. Wright, *Mission of God*, 191–92.
89. Schnabel, *Paul the Missionary*, 210.
90. Luther, *Commentary*, 30.

horrible punishment for Jesus's own sin cannot be good news for the world. Therefore, Apostle Paul mentioned, "We preach Christ crucified, a stumbling block to Jews and folly to Gentiles" (1 Cor 1:23).

The gospel did not come from a cultural vacuum, but it came through the brutal execution of Jesus on the cross by the shedding of his blood. Though the message of the cross has come to us as a word of life and liberation, Burmese Buddhists and Nat worship respond quite differently. For them, the crucifixion of Christ represents the most brutal and violent death. Though Christians have pointed to the cross as a solution, the Burmese Buddhists are bewildered by such brutal execution as a solution for human suffering.

When asked about life after death, "the Buddha expressly refuses to answer questions relative to life after death, he condemns all speculation as unedifying,"[91] which means there is no gospel in Buddhism and Nat worship, as in Christianity. So, what is a legitimate response for Christian missionaries toward the Burmese Nat worship? The concept of suffering has been misinterpreted and misunderstood in the Burmese context because suffering is the result of one's previous fault. Hence, the suffering of Christ is his own fault in the eyes of the Burmese people. Sacrifice is not a mistake but is based on a cause-and-effect relation.[92]

The Christian gospel is not reversed back to the law, and human beings are undeserved and unlovable, yet the suffering of Christ produced the good news for sinners and enemies. The search for ways to escape suffering in Buddhism through the four noble truths and eightfold path failed.[93] In other words, the Buddha died but has not risen; Christ died and has risen. The power of the gospel lies in his resurrection from the dead. Therefore, the gospel Paul preached was authentic because the risen Lord Jesus Christ gave it.[94] The power of the gospel of Christ compelled Paul to rethink everything from the other way around, to see that the Jews and Gentiles are alike.

The power of the gospel enabled Paul to change his religion, and the Jew became a Christian.[95] Paul introduces himself as "a servant of Christ Jesus,

---

91. Coomaraswamy, *Buddha and Gospel*, 120.
92. Heim, *Saved from Sacrifice*, 45.
93. Coomaraswamy, *Buddha and Gospel*, 40.
94. Senior and Stuhmueller, *Biblical Foundations*, 167.
95. Senior and Stuhmueller, *Biblical Foundations*, 167.

called to be an apostle and set apart for the gospel of God" (Rom 1:1 NIV). The power of Jesus Christ's resurrection set Paul apart to preach it. Paul's commitment to preaching the gospel from his conversion was the dominant and determinative focus of his whole life.[96] Likewise, Judson boldly proclaimed to the Burmese king, "There is One Being who exists eternally, and beside Him, there is no other God."[97] Just as Paul conceived that the Corinthians, Athenians, and other citizens in his missionary journey followed false religious practice, Judson stated that the Burmese Nat worship was an atheistic and false religious practice. Edward Judson asserted:

> As Mr. Judson will not have time to write you by this opportunity, I will endeavor to give you some idea of our situation here and of our plans and prospects. We have found the country, as we expected in a most deplorable state, full of darkness, idolatry, and cruelty – full of commotion and uncertainty. What means did Judson use in his endeavor to bring about this great moral and spiritual revolution? Simply the gospel of Christ. The sole weapons of his warfare were the old-fashioned truths, the existence of a personal and beneficent God, the fatal sinfulness of man, and salvation by faith in the Son of God, who came to seek and save that which was lost.[98]

The gospel of Christ is powerful enough to break through the power of Nat spirits and explain suffering in the context of Myanmar. The content of the gospel is very different from the content of the alternative explanation of suffering as portrayed in Burmese Nat worship. The power of the gospel was a prefigurative divine plan of God demonstrated in the life of Abraham to sacrifice his own son Isaac. However, God substituted with a lamb on Mt. Moriah (Gen 22:1–2). The God who commanded Abraham to sacrifice his son is the same God who saved Isaac by providing a substitutionary atonement. This is just one part of the dimensions of the power of the gospel. As the human victim must provide the sacrificial animal in the context of Burmese Nat worship, there is no divine power involved in the process of sacrifice. It

---

96. Köstenberger and O'Brien, *Salvation*, 173.
97. Bailey, *Adoniram Judson*, 61.
98. Judson, *Life of Adoniram Judson*, 82.

is essential to understand that to accept and believe in the gospel is to let the grace of God work in us. Schnabel writes:

> Before Paul became a Christian and a missionary, he persecuted Christians. As an envoy from the Jewish authorities in Jerusalem, he knew something about power – political power that was capable of eliminating dissenters, social and cultural power that pressured people to conform to traditions and customs as long-held beliefs, legal power that was in a position to punish troublemakers. Paul met the risen Lord Jesus Christ on the road to Damascus – an encounter that he had not sought, but whose reality and meaning he could not deny, an encounter whose significance changed his life. Paul became an apostle because of the risen Lord and because the power of God was present in his preaching.[99]

Only God can cause the Burmese people to accept and believe a message that seems scandalous and nonsensical. Only God's Spirit can create space and use people to preach the gospel. There has been a discussion whether the core message of the gospel is the forgiveness of sin or social justice. Johannes Nissen writes:

> This is a discussion not only among biblical scholars but also among missiologists. Thus, the evangelists have asked the ecumenical the question, "Do you weep for the lost?" However, the counter-question from the ecumenical is "Do you weep for the poor?" . . . some Christians wish to preach a gospel of sociopolitical liberation to the poor, whereas the others want to offer forgiveness of sins to the rich.[100]

There is a great debate between the social gospel and the gospel in Christianity. In other words, the perspective of the gospel between evangelical and liberal Christians is quite different. For example, a Myanmar theologian loosely put it, "the people of Myanmar responded to the gospel from their perspective backgrounds. The Burmese Buddhists have a religious approach/response while other ethnic groups have a cultural approach/response to the

---

99. Schnabel, *Paul the Missionary*, 451–52.
100. Nissen, *New Testament and Mission*, 66.

Christian gospel."[101] In the same vein, Heim stated, "What if they take different approaches so long as they reach the same destination."[102]

Second, the gospel is full of grace.[103] One of the most important concepts we will find in the Bible to understand and apply daily to ourselves is the grace of God. If we do not understand the meaning of the grace of God, we will not understand the gospel because we are to proclaim "the gospel of the grace of God" (Acts 20:24). Not only are we saved by grace through faith in Christ, but also, we are to "grow in grace and knowledge of our Lord" (2 Pet 3:18). God's grace sustains us and contains strength when we are weak (2 Cor 12:9). When we are needy, we are invited to come to God's throne of grace to "receive mercy and find grace to help in time of need" (Heb 4:16). There are many dimensions in the gospel, but the writer emphasizes the power and grace of the gospel in this section.

Without a proper understanding of the meaning of grace, one cannot identify with Christ, who graciously gave his life for the ransom of many. Grace helps us to understand the violence and brutal execution of Jesus and his blood on the cross as a result of grace, love, and mercy, but not as a threat as the Burmese Buddhists view it. The teachings of the Buddha forbid killing even a tiny insect. Therefore, there is no other way than to embrace Nat worship for the Burmese Buddhists to explain suffering for good. So, the witch-masters take responsibility for the guilt of others by explaining and acting as the scapegoat for violence against the innocent people so that there are no consequences. However, on the other hand, the witch-masters sometimes fail to deliver their clients from suffering due to their incompetency and the insufficiency of their clients' offerings. In such cases, the clients must increase the amount or size of the offering, assuming that Nat is still unpleasant with the clients. But conversely, there are no such things as an ineffective or incompetent sacrifice in Jesus Christ because there is divine power in it.

Grace is the cause of Christ's death because humans cannot save themselves; therefore, full of grace, mercy, and loving-kindness, Jesus was sacrificed in place of humankind. So, knowing the cause of Jesus's death on the cross enables us to accept the price he paid for our sins. Our wages were death,

---

101. Price, Sepulveda, and Smith, eds., *Mission Matters*.
102. Heim, *Salvations*, 130.
103. Newbigin, *Gospel*, 175.

but Jesus paid the price for us (Rom 6:23). There is no such thing as grace in Nat worship, but karmic law is a kind of reciprocal relationship between the people and the Nat in the Burmese context. The writer means that if you do not offer something, Nat will do nothing for you. Moreover, you must first make offerings so that Nat may give you your requests. In contrast, God makes the offering first and humans need to accept it.

The Suffering Church

It is appropriate to begin by asking, how can we understand the existence of suffering with the existence of an all-loving, all-wise, all-powerful creator God?[104] More especially, why are the children of God suffering? One concrete reason for the suffering church is proclaiming the gospel truth. This suffering occurs when one attempts to achieve God's purposes in addressing that something is wrong with human beings. And God takes the initiative that suffering shall not have the last word, but that victory is the result of proclaiming the gospel and conversion from paganism to Christianity. Since its inauguration, the church in Myanmar encountered sufferings from two sources, Buddhism and liberal Christianity. The Scripture portrays the suffering of the church several times, for instance, in the life of Stephen as follows:

> Now those who had been scattered by the persecution that broke out when Stephen was killed traveled as far as Phoenicia, Cyprus, and Antioch, spreading the word only among Jews. News of this reached the church in Jerusalem, and they sent Barnabas to Antioch. When he arrived and saw what the grace of God had done, he was glad and encouraged them all to remain true to the Lord with all their hearts. (Acts 11:19, 22–23 NIV)

Judson began suffering persecution from the Burmese Nat worshipers and the Buddhist government when he converted Burmese Nat-Buddhists to Christianity in Myanmar. On one occasion, Judson boldly asked his language teacher:

> Do you believe all that is contained in the book of St. Matthew that I have given you? In particular do you believe that the Son of God died on the cross? "Ah you caught me now," the old

---

104. Gooding and Lennox, *Suffering Life's Pain*, 149.

teacher admitted, "I believe that He suffered death. But I cannot admit He suffered the shameful death of the cross." Then he said: "as you utter those words, I see my error. I have been trusting my word reasons, not in the word of God. I now believe the crucifixion of Christ, because it is contained in the Scripture. I think I shall not be lost even though I should die suddenly. Why because I love Jesus Christ."[105]

Judson suffered insurmountable tortures, imprisonment, countless trials, and death for the sake of Christ and salvation for the Burmese people. During his seventeenth year of imprisonment, "Judson's hair and neck [were] filthy, his arms sore from the cut of the cord, his ankles already chafed raw from the three pairs of heavy iron fetters on his elevated feet."[106] Every true Christian admitted it is difficult to be a Christian in Myanmar.

Conversely, Fr. Vincentius Sangermano, a Roman Catholic missionary, had never experienced persecution from the Burmese government during his ministry in Myanmar. He expressed, "Christianity has hitherto experienced no persecution."[107] As the previous chapter mentioned, Sangermano's reputation grew following the establishment of St. Paul School and other social services in Myanmar, and he had not met with direct persecution. It was simply because Sangermano did not attempt to convert the Burmese to the Catholic faith.

However, Judson expressed how much joy and reward he had in spite of toil with tears as a result of the gospel of Matthew being completed in May 1817. Judson gave a Burmese man the translation of the gospel of Matthew and a gospel tract, "A View of the Christian Religion." One should not forget the early Christians' expression that the present sufferings were not worth comparing with the glories to be enjoyed eternally.

In the context of Burmese Nat worship, how do we talk about suffering from a Christian perspective? Liberal Christians in Myanmar turn to Gutierrez's concept of liberation, which aims to mitigate the exploitation of the capitalists of the poor workers and the injustice done to the poor.[108]

---

105. Anderson, *To the Golden Shore*, 241.
106. Anderson, *To the Golden Shore*, 314.
107. Trager, *Burma through Alien Eyes*, 10.
108. Gutierrez, *Theology of Liberation*, 110.

Liberation theology was born when the Christian faith confronted the social injustice done to the poor, marginalized, and ethnic minorities.[109] Gustavo Gutierrez, one of the fathers of liberation theology, contends that a theology of liberation is an answer to historical salvation and human liberation from social injustice.[110] On the one hand, the social suffering of the people in Myanmar opens an opportunity for sharing the gospel; on the other, too much focus on the social needs of the people can deviate from the mission of God.

Oftentimes, such a response to social issues can be assumed as the norm for the mission of God. In line with this, a German missiologist, Sundermeier, coined "convivence" as a way of doing a mission toward injustice in a socioeconomic community. For him, alleviating social poverty and helping each other equates the mission of God.[111]

In order to avoid persecution from Buddhism, Simon Pau Khan En shifts approaches by employing Christ as a liberator for the socioeconomic poor, and Christianity as a means to engage in dialogue with Buddhism. He adds, "To present Jesus Christ as a liberator at this level, the Christians in Myanmar have to engage in dialogue with the Buddhists and make an attempt to articulate how Jesus ends those series of existence (*samsara*) by carrying vicariously all the sufferings (*dukkha*) caused by deeds (*Kamma*) in the series of existence."[112] The researcher discovered that the liberal Christians in Myanmar realized the richness of Buddhist culture and tradition and the negative impact of Western Christian missionaries on ethnic groups' religious practice, leading to the conclusion that interfaith dialogue is necessary.[113]

Interpreting Christ as a liberator at the socioeconomic and cultural level to achieve coexistence with other faiths largely minimizes the framework of a Trinitarian *missio Dei*. The content of the Christian gospel is very different from the content of liberation and the alternative explanation for suffering in Burmese Nat Buddhism. When the teaching of the Buddha does not provide cessation or liberation from suffering, Buddhists opt for the alternative explanation from the Nat worship principles. The alternative explanation for

---

109. Boff and Boff, *Introducing Liberation Theology*, 3.
110. Gutierrez, *Theology of Liberation*, 29.
111. Kisskalt, "Mission as Convivence," 6.
112. En, *Nat Worship*, 239.
113. Si, *God in Burma*, 107.

suffering in Burmese Nat worship has two (upper and lower) paths, whereas the content of the Christian explanation for suffering is possible only through the redemptive work of Jesus Christ.[114] There is a huge difference between the concept of suffering and salvation in Burmese Nat Buddhism and Christianity. Buddhists do not believe in the concept of a savior or salvation through someone else. The biblical understanding of the grace of God is that Jesus Christ, as the Lamb of God, died on the cross to take away the moral evil of the world.[115]

The former caused the church suffering because they diverted the meaning of the gospel into the social gospel; as a result, there is dissent and division among Christians in Myanmar. This will lead to the next discussion – Christian suffering under the Buddhist military government in Myanmar. It is necessary to make mention of Adoniram Judson when the suffering of Christianity is discussed under the military government in Myanmar.

On 23 May 1824, the British arrived in Burma and took Rangoon. It was on 8 June 1824, while Judson and his wife had dinner at home that unexpectedly, a man with a spotted face entered their humble home. "The king wants you!" he said roughly and cast Judson to the ground, bound him and dragged him from his home. Geiseman writes, "Suffering the agonizing torments of helplessness, an outraged wife pleads for mercy, offers gifts, cries, begs, insists, commands – but all in vain."[116] Although things did not look promising for the missionary in Burma, Judson continued teaching the word of God. Judson was imprisoned for seventeen months in one of the cruelest jails in the world.[117] The military junta leaders recently detained Hkalam Samson, a Kachin Christian leader, on 4 December 2022 Mandalay International Airport, Radio Free Asia reported.[118] A Christian pastor who did not want to be named for security reasons, said that Dr. Samson has been banned from leaving the country.

When Myanmar gained independence from the British in 1948, Aung San persuaded the Chin, Kachin, Shan, and other ethnic nationalities to join the Union of Myanmar with a policy based on the principles of nation-building

---

114. Parratt, *Reader in African*, 102.
115. Schaeffer, *How Should We?*, 55.
116. Geiseman, *Men and Missions*, 117.
117. Judson, *Life of Adoniram Judson*, 111.
118. Radio Free Asia, updated at 2:19 p.m. EST on 5 December 2022.

and unity in diversity. However, after Aung San was assassinated, U Nu adopted the state religion of Buddhism as a means of "national integration."[119] Christians' persecution in Myanmar had happened before its independence from the British. However, the persecution of Christianity flared up when U Nu, the prime minister, reversed Aung San's vision of national integration as a strategy for nation-building.

Moreover, Christianity is a minority religion in Myanmar, yet a majority religion of the ethnic minorities in the country. However, the notion of religious-oriented traditional Burmese nationalism intertwined with the Myanmar national identity, as an old saying so clearly put: *Buddha bta, Myanmar lumyo* (to be a Myanmar is to be a Buddhist). In other words, the Myanmar government officials have the right to persecute minority religions such as Christianity and Islam. The author witnessed on many occasions that the military government uses its personnel to marry Christian women and has other means of forcible conversion to Buddhism. There are restrictions on church-building and religious organizing, forced labor conscription, killings, torture, rape, abductions, and other acts of violence against Christianity. Looking at the relationship between ethnic minorities and ethnic majorities, foreign missionaries and locals, and Christian relationships with people of other faiths, ecumenical Christians employ dialogue as a model for reconciliation. In the following section, the author continues from where he left off the discussion about the dissent and division among Christians in Myanmar.

Due to the two reasons mentioned above for the cause of Christian suffering, Myanmar liberal Christians developed interreligious dialogue as a paradigm shift to approach radical Burmese Buddhists. In the same vein, Lesslie Newbigin, a missionary to southern India, became concerned about the increasing religious pluralism in India, and believed that religious pluralists such as Paul Knitter overlooked the urgent need for human unity amidst the peculiarity of the church. As a result, interreligious dialogue is the means which Christians employ to avoid persecution and suffering. Newbigin rightly pointed out that "The problem is that we want unity on our terms, and it is our rival programs for unity which tear us apart. The very heart of the biblical

---

119. Sakhong, *In Defense of Identity*, 46.

vision for the unity of humankind is that its center is not an imperial power but the slain Lamb."[120]

As opposed to Knitter, who believed that a shift must occur from Christianity to all religions as the center of God, Newbigin believed that action for justice and peace in the world is a secondary matter. It is not the heart of the mission.[121] According to Newbigin, "For those who have shared in the multifaith, multiculture, multirace world of today, it seems preposterous to maintain that in all infinite pluralities and relativities of human affairs there should be one absolute against which everything else is to be measured."[122] In other words, Newbigin believes in the Christian history of redemption revealed in the Scripture and preserved by the church as the center of our witness to our non-Christian neighbors. If a church ceases to be a missional church, it has lost the essential character of the Church.[123]

Ethnic Christian minorities in a Buddhist majority country in Myanmar have had to endure double suffering. While Christianity is a minority religion in the country, it is a majority religion of the ethnic minorities such as Chin, Kachin, Karen, and Kayah. Politically these ethnic minorities – the Chin, Kachin, Karen, and Kayah – face an identity crisis, and religiously, these minorities which are Christian face persecution from the Buddhist government. As a result, liberal Christian leaders in Myanmar propose peace and social justice as the answer to the problem Myanmar Christians have faced for half a century.

A Myanmar liberal Christian leader asserts that, "the chief obstacle to any meaningful inter-faith dialogue in Myanmar, to the best of my observation, has been and still is the Christians' unhealthy self-righteous holier-than-thou pietism and attitude toward non-Christians who are disdainfully looked upon as a bunch of hell-bound, godless peoples."[124] For Myanmar liberal Christians, an unChristian-like attitude rooted in a narrow understanding of the meaning of being a Christian is the leading cause of Christian suffering.

---

120. Newbigin, *Gospel*, 159.
121. Newbigin, *Gospel*, 135.
122. Newbigin, *Gospel*, 157.
123. Ott, Strauss, and Tennent, *Encountering Theology*, 193.
124. Za Bik, "Universal Salvation," 24.

The question remains as to how we present Jesus as the only way for eternal life while Christianity suffered persecution politically and religiously. An orthodox Buddhist's view of attaining nirvana – heaven – is that this occurs through human knowledge or good deeds, while Christians believe it is by grace through faith in Christ alone.

According to a Myanmar Christian leader, the two views, knowledge or good deeds and faith, may co-exist in Myanmar on the grounds of the New Year Water Festival.[125] The Myanmar New Year water festival signifies threefold meanings: the myth of the visit of *Thakyamin* [Nat]; the ceremonial hair-washing, and the feast itself.[126] If Christians comply with the New Year water festival of Myanmar Buddhists, they may co-exist peacefully so that Christians avoid suffering from persecutions. Do Sian Thang asserts that the water festival symbolizes the theological concept of redemption, expressed by the Israelite New Year Festival, water baptism, and the Eucharist. However, the researcher concludes that the gospel of Jesus Christ has to transform the concept of the New Year Festival into Easter and Christmas because the New Year Festival embodies Nat worship, whereas Easter and Christmas demonstrate the love of God.

The pressures on Christianity in Myanmar are unpredictable; therefore, liberal Christians mentioned above have attempted to avoid conflict with the Burmese Buddhist government by implementing interreligious dialogue. The researcher argues that interreligious dialogue is a secondary matter, as Lesslie Newbigin noted, and he insists that "religion is not the means of salvation."[127] The researcher argues that all such claims regarding interreligious dialogue, peaceful coexistence, and social justice negated the message of Jesus Christ, the crucified Lord who rose again into glory. The preceding discussion focused on the destiny of the individual's soul after death. Newbigin states, "The urgent question is not: how shall I be saved? But: How shall God's name be hallowed, His Kingdom come, His will be done on earth as in heaven?"[128] In other words, how we present salvation is of utmost importance in a pluralistic society.

---

125. Thang, "Toward a Theology," 27.
126. Thang, "Toward a Theology," 24.
127. Newbigin, *Open Secret*, 177.
128. Newbigin, *Signs Amid Rubble*, 71. See also Newbigin, *Gospel*, 171.

The Role of Nat Worship Informs Life in Society

In response to the prevalence of Nat worship in the socioeconomic and religiopolitical life of the people, Simon Pau Khan En squarely bases his approach on his article "Building an Eco-Just Society." He states that "the statues and images exhibited in the West at city squares and public centers have exposed the picture of human beings, while in the east the arts have revealed the beauty of nature, landscape, forest, trees, rivers, etc. This is what determined theology in general and the doctrine of salvation in particular."[129]

En claims that the "Judeo-Christian soteriology primarily designed and formulated in the west mainly focused on human salvation, while the oriental religions mainly appreciate nature, the manifestations, and revelation of the deity through nature."[130] En presses on to say that the Western-oriented doctrine of salvation lacks the nature aspect in the Eastern-oriented doctrine of salvation. En's emphasis on human salvation through eco-justification includes the universal aspect of salvation, the whole scope of salvation known as ecological soteriology. S. Mark Heim argues that salvation is a relationship of communion through Christ with God and with other creatures. According to his view, salvation is not just about being forgiven for sins, but also about being restored to a right relationship with God.[131]

In his article "Universal Salvation," Edmund Za Bik argues, based on the divine economy of God's salvific plan, that salvation is open to anyone who does the will of the Father or who follows the way of Christ. Za Bik's emphasis is based on John 14:6 that whoever does the *will* of the Father and whoever follows the *way* of Christ will be saved.[132] However, for Za Bik, the meaning of John 14:6 is to imitate the true *identity* and *being* of Christ by questioning, "What constitutes a person's real being or identity?" In short, Za Bik argues that the person's identity is not in the name. For example, he adds that Jesus is the same as Joshua, Jeshua, and Jeshuah. The meaning is "Jehovah is salvation," later changed to "Jesus" and given to the son of Joseph and Mary (Matt 1:21; Luke 1:31).[133] Za Bik asserts that "if a name is an indicator or identity of

---

129. En, "Eco-Just Society," 54.
130. En, "Eco-Just Society," 54.
131. Heim, *Depth of Riches*, 59.
132. Za Bik, "Universal Salvation," 24.
133. Za Bik, "Universal Salvation," 27.

the name-bearer at all, it would follow, logically speaking, then that anyone with the name *Maung Maung* will have the same ontological whatness or being or identity."[134]

According to Za Bik, it is evident that it is not a name that constitutes a person's real identity but the *how* (way of life) and what (essence/being) which are put together. The way of life consists of love and justice, and we do not know God by his name but by his way of life.[135] In other words, doing social justice is the way of life for Za Bik. The researcher argues that John 14:6, "I am the Way, the Truth and the Life" means Jesus is the Way to the Father (way of life), the Truth is the Word, and the Life is eternal life. New Testament scholar Craig Keener argues that John 14:6 is what "Jesus answers Thomas's question thus: The Father is where I am going, and I am how you will get there."[136]

When the Judsons began journeying to the Southeast Asian country, they had heard that Myanmar was what they called "heathen superstition."[137] The first American Baptist missionary Judson stated the prevalence of an ancient religion – that Nat worship is deeply fixed in the hearts and habits of Myanmar.[138]

Nat worship is a primal religion that the Burmese majority and the ethnic minorities had practiced long before the foreign religions Buddhism and Christianity were imported to the country. Since Nat worship is an indigenous religion in Myanmar, it informs life in all dimensions including socioeconomic and religiopolitical life. Nat worship embraces and enriches the moral elements of religious practice and the economic welfare of society. Nat worship became an underlying web of religiosity by which the Burmese people could comprehend socioeconomic and religiopolitical life. Nat worship is, therefore, deeply interwoven with the Burmese Buddhist government.

Hence, Nat worship plays a crucial role for the people of Myanmar. One of the toughest kings, Anawratha, tried to replace Nat worship with Theravada Buddhism, but he failed.[139] As previously mentioned, Buddhism slowly came

---

134. Za Bik, "Universal Salvation," 27.
135. Za Bik, "Universal Salvation," 29.
136. Keener, *IVP Bible Background*, 291.
137. Kaloyanides, "Show Us," p. 1.
138. Judson, *Life of Adoniram Judson*, 81.
139. Ray, *Theravada Buddhism*, 150.

to tolerate Nat worship, with the result that the Burmese Buddhists place a Nat shrine side-by-side with the Buddha images in their houses. Nat worship and Theravada Buddhism are two sides of the same coin for Myanmar. There is a reciprocal benefit from the amalgamation of Buddhism and Nat worship. For instance, the Burmese Buddhists secure a better future from the benevolence of Nat worship. Through sacrificial offering Nat worshipers attain fortunes so that, in turn, they can perform good deeds to the needy in society. Technically, the Burmese Buddhists worship two gods, Nat for the security of this worldly life and the Buddha for a better circle of rebirth in the life hereafter.[140] We will discuss the life hereafter in the next section.

Life after Death

When the Buddha was asked about life after death, "the Buddha expressly refuses to answer question relative to life after death, he condemns all speculation as unedifying," which means that there is no true gospel in Buddhism.[141] In Buddhism, nothing is permanent. To make the point clear, in Buddhism, there is no eternal existence that comes from heaven or that will transmigrate or proceed straight to heaven or hell after death.[142] Conversely, one of the significant beliefs in Nat worship is the existence of life after death. The concept of the existence of life after death in Nat worship fits into Christianity. However, there is a vastly different interpretation of life after death between Nat worship and Christianity. According to the Burmese Nat worship system, all the spirits of the dead are not going to the heavenly realm.

The question is how the spirit of the deceased gets to the heavenly abode. The Burmese Nat worshipers and Buddhists believe that the deceased spirit cannot go directly to the abode without crossing the running stream. In their belief, there is a gatekeeper at the stream, so they put some coins in the hands of the dead body for the payment of his ferry-toll.[143] Similarly, for the Zomi people in Myanmar, called *Han ken*, meaning – *fetches to the cemetery* – when a person dies, either domestic or wild animals, like a cow, buffalo, mithun, elephant, and pig had to be slain at the funeral. This was

---

140. Nash, *Practicing Ethnography*, 86.
141. Coomaraswamy, *Buddha and Gospel*, 120.
142. Dhammananda, *What Buddhists Believe*, 115.
143. En, *Nat Worship*, 72.

done so that the deceased spirits would be accompanied by the slain animals and the gatekeeper would allow them to go to the abode. The belief in life after death in Nat worship endorses Burmese Buddhists in two ways: (1) the belief in body and soul, and (2) the belief in someone's help to get to the abode or an eternal place.

Even though the Buddhists believe that an eternal soul is a misconception of the human conscience, by embracing the Burmese Nat worship they believe that the heavenly realm is where the human soul goes after death. Not only that, that abode cannot be reached without the help of someone and the payment to enter it. In this sense, the Burmese Nat worship becomes the *praeparatio evangelica* for the Burmese Buddhists to accept Christianity. However, Simon Pau Khan En, author of *Nat Worship*, observes only the surface of the concept of soteriology in Nat worship. Furthermore, he suggests that "one can say that the concept of relief or salvation [that] exists in Nat worship is to do with physical aspects and has nothing to do with spiritual salvation."[144] En continues, "The biblical concept of salvation includes both the physical and the spiritual in its wholeness, so that human beings will enjoy salvation in this life, *here – and – now*, and in the next life, hereafter."[145] The problem with liberal Christians in Myanmar is the emphasis on physical salvation in the *here and now* over the hereafter. There is a contrasting view between the present age and the age to come in Christianity. Paul would agree that the righteous suffering in this world will be greatly rewarded. Therefore, the present suffering of Christians in this world is meaningful, as Paul stated below.

Paul believed and taught that there is life after death. He rightly asserts, "If the Spirit of him who raised Jesus from the dead dwells in you, he who raised Christ Jesus from the dead will give life to your mortal bodies also through his Sprit which dwells in you" (Rom 8:11). Paul preached about the connection between the resurrection of Jesus and believers particularly in 1 Corinthians 15:12–14: "Now if Christ is preached as raised from the dead, how can some of you say that there is no resurrection of the dead? if Christ has not been raised, our preaching is in vain, and your faith is in vain." Apostle Paul speaks of Jesus Christ, who had abolished death and brought life through the gospel.[146]

---

144. En, *Nat Worship*, 125.
145. En, *Nat Worship*, 125.
146. Hodges, *Systematic Theology*, 711.

Religious Ceremony

In this section, the researcher selects one typical ritual ceremony, *Shinbyu*, the Burmese term for a novitiation ceremony which is regarded as one of the most sacred rituals in Myanmar. We can learn basic meanings from this ritual ceremony, as Charles H. Kraft put it – separation, transition, and incorporation.[147] In a Burmese Nat-Buddhist society, the individual who entered the *Shinbyu* first was removed from society, isolated for about three months and finally returned to society. The basic concept of *Shinbyu* is similar to Christian ordination. The candidates for *Shinbyu* stay in the monastery for about three months; during this period, the boys experience the rigors of an orthodox Buddhist monastic lifestyle that involves celibacy, formal voluntary poverty, absolute nonviolence, and daily fasting between noon and the following sunrise. As a Buddhist monastic life, *Shinbyu* required a removal from society for a period of time, there is also, according to Paul, a requirement for Christians to be set apart from the pattern of the world not for a period of time but the whole life. There are three aspects of the Christian life that are worthy of consideration.

First, when Paul is aware of the divine calling to be the servant of Christ, he wants to emphasize why he is called to be removed from the pattern of the world (Rom 1:1). "Set apart" is a phrase Paul often used after his conversion. Paul considered his firsthand experience as a call to preach the gospel to the Gentiles. Paul's words in Romans 1:15–16, "'when he who had set me apart before I was born' echo Jeremiah 1:4–5 and Isaiah 49:6."[148] Paul was separated by God to teach and proclaim the good news of salvation in Christ. David M. Kasali contends, "he was ordained by Jesus and never lost sight of his mission."[149]

In a pluralistic society such as Myanmar, setting apart from paganism is necessary to defend the Christian faith. For example, Christians must decide whether they can participate in the *Shinbyu* ritual ceremony when it is considered a social obligation.[150] As the *Shinbyu* individual is to be removed from society for a while and return to society to give witness to a monastic

---

147. Kraft, *Anthropology for Christian Witness*, 209.
148. Senior and Stuhlmueller, *Biblical Foundations*, 166.
149. Adeyemo, *African Bible Commentary*, 1377.
150. Nissen, *New Testament and Mission*, 121.

lifestyle in the community, living a transformed life in the church and society is necessary for believers. As the *Shinbyu* boy is separated from society, Paul set apart himself for the gospel of Jesus and incorporated with the Gentiles by proclaiming that salvation is for all.

Second, a living sacrifice in Christianity may refer to a transition from being a child to being a mature or adult Christian. The individual candidate experiences the rigors of an orthodox Buddhist monastic lifestyle that involves celibacy, formal voluntary poverty, absolute nonviolence, and daily fasting during this period. There is a similar lifestyle in a Christian context, but for Paul, it means living a transformed life in the church and society. Paul emphasizes, as Adeyemo has explained, a living "sacrifice as the renewing of your mind especially the internal process, a reorientation of our world view as we seek to live the way Christ lived and to think as he thought."[151] This is the most difficult part of the Christian life as we ought to leave the pattern of this world and transition into a new Christian community.

When a person is in Christ, they are a new creature (2 Cor 5:17). Issiaka Coulibaly asserts, "in other words, we no longer live as we did before because we live for Jesus Christ who gives new meaning to our lives."[152] The underlying emphasis of apostle Paul in his letter is the need for renewal of character so that believers become Christlike and grow in sanctification. If the faith claimed does not affect our worldview, that faith is in vain, and the so-called believer will forfeit rewards in heaven. In this sense, Paul's worldview was changed. Paul realized Jesus of Nazareth, who had been crucified, was both for the Jew and Gentile and he was convinced that Jesus Christ had risen from the dead.[153] As a result, compared to his pre-Christian experience Paul rethinks everything from the ground up.

Third, by expressing a deep awareness of his obligation to preach the gospel to the Gentiles, Paul is bridging the communication barrier between Jews and Gentiles by incorporating salvation by grace through faith in Christ alone. In this, we see the boundary-shattering as the gospel moves incrementally from the Jewish to a multicultural context, non-Jewish. In other words, Paul emphasizes that God's presence is not tied to the Jewish temple.

---

151. Kasali,"Romans," 1395.
152. Coulibaly, "2 Corinthians," 1430.
153. Senior and Stuhlmueller, *Biblical Foundations*, 168.

God is with all the people outside Jerusalem (Acts 7:1–38). Paul emphasizes that faith in the gospel of Christ overcomes racial, physical, cultural, and geographical barriers.[154] However, incorporating people of other faiths in a pluralistic context can be very challenging. For example, at the dawn of Christianity, the Burmese Nat worshipers and Buddhists regarded baptism not as a sacrament in a Christian sense but as a civic duty or the integration of Western social identity.[155] In the same way, the Western missionaries could not understand the meaning of the Burmese ritual ceremony and interpreted it on their own, using Western explanations and elaborations. Syncretism can occur easily within religious ceremonial activities. Therefore, the power of the gospel plays a crucial role in the transformed life of the church and its community. This will lead to the following discussion of sacred and profane.

Sacred and Profane in Nat Worship

Sacred and profane play important roles in the religious and spiritual landscape in Southeast Asia in general and Myanmar in particular. The biblical meaning of sacred and profane becomes clear within the context of Nat worship. For example, novitiation or *Shinbyu* candidates are temporarily separated from all worldly attachments, including a group of peers, societal identity, and affairs of mundane life.[156] The concept of religious sacred, which is also found in Nat worship, broadens the significance of a missiological approach in a twofold way. First, it indicates the separation of sacred from profane, and second, there is a solid reason why certain places are sacred or holy, and others are profane.[157]

First, in Genesis 2:15, God put Adam in the garden of Eden to take care of it. Munther Isaac argues that the concept of sanctuary, covenant, and promised land originated from the garden of Eden.[158] Genesis 2:3 and Exodus 20:8 indicates that a holy God requires us to make holy time and space where we can worship and glorify him. Therefore, for the people of Israel, God sanctified the seventh day as a time to worship him and provided Canaan

---

154. Flemming, *Contextualization*, 35.
155. Young, *Vain Debates*, 38–39.
156. St. John, *Victor Turner*, 128.
157. Allerton, "Introduction," 234–51.
158. Isaac, *From Land to Lands*, xv.

as a place to worship and glorify him. In other words, God set apart the sacred from the profane. God is very concerned about a place and time for his children to worship him. The significant difference between Nat worship and Christianity on sacred and profane is that the former is temporary and the latter, Christianity, permanent.

Before the reign of King Anawratha in Myanmar, Mt. Popa was the abode of the Nat, *Min Mahagiri*. The king imposed laws to remove Nat shrines from Mt. Popa, but the people secretly brought them to their houses as guardians of Nat. As a result, houses became the center of Nat worship. Hence, the Nat shrines were set up alongside the Buddha's image. In the Burmese Nat worship context, the vital significance of the family altar and family worship is a point of contact in sharing the gospel of Christ.[159]

The holy God of Israel is often separated from what is not holy, yet he took the initiative to fellowship with humanity. As a result, the promised land for his people in the Old Testament is portrayed as a sacred place set apart for the chosen nation, Israel. So, Israel is called the holy land (Ezek 45:4). Spirits (Nat) also occupied specific locations, including trees, caves, rivers, mountains, and rocks in Myanmar. Although the concept seems similar in a religious sense of the term, the biblical meaning of sacred and profane has a deeper meaning than that of Nat worship.

Second, there is a concrete reason for the sacredness and profanity of certain locations. It is because of the presence of a holy God or spirits and its direct relation to the people living in it. The land must be holy for Israel because it functions as a social center for God's people.[160] In the same way, the Burmese Buddhists and Nat worshipers believed that Nat identified themselves with certain landscapes and people in many ways. For example, as previously mentioned, Mt. Popa is a sacred place for the Nat (spirits) but then there was a shift to houses as sacred places. Certain locations are recognized as holy because the spirits who reside there are connected to the people. However, biblically, holy lands are understood to be under the sphere of the reign of God.[161]

---

159. En, *Nat Worship*, 394.
160. Isaac, *From Land to Lands*, 55.
161. Isaac, *From Land to Lands*, 347.

Victor Turner uses liminality as a lens to examine the meaning of religious rituals that divide sacred and profane. The term "liminality" refers to the mid-phase of rituals during which the participants are neither here nor there (participants are transitioning from one society to another), but genuinely in between distinctions.[162] In Christianity, sacred living or sanctification is the beginning of a lifelong process of being continually shaped into the likeness of Christ. Unlike Victor Turner's concept of liminality, there is no such thing in Christianity that one is in between, neither here nor there.

In other words, there is not the mid-phase of saved or unsaved in Christianity, where one is in between heaven or hell. Although holiness is often seen in contrast to profanity or uncleanliness, God takes the initiative in drawing people to realize his eternal purpose. Therefore, "holiness is the common ground on which communion between God and his people is actualized. Holiness is often seen as something contagious, humans and things become holy from contact with the holy God."[163] In other words, when people are associated with God, they are described as holy. In the same way, the person who is consecrated to serve the holy God is also expected to exhibit the sanctified life.

---

162. St. John, *Victor Turner*, 128.
163. Dyrness and Karkkainen, *Global Dictionary*, 789.

CHAPTER 3

Research Approach, Design, and Procedures

To obtain the answers to the research questions, the researcher used a qualitative methodology[1] using two methodologies: library research and structured interview. The researcher collected data regarding contemporary Myanmar Christianity, theology of mission, and mission of God, by accessing more than one hundred books, dissertations, journal articles with the help of the library of Concordia Theological Seminary Fort Wayne. In addition, the researcher gathered data regarding Burmese Nat worship and Burmese Buddhism, from about fifty books, dissertations, and journal articles.

In order to learn about the pervasiveness of Burmese Nat worship and Burmese Buddhism, structured interview via face-to-face and survey [email] was conducted. Emma Dahlin recently explored new methods for researching increasingly digitalized societies – electronic research methods such as email interviews.[2] Although Sue McHale states that "email has been widely used for more than a decade, its value as an interview technique has not been thoroughly reviewed and assessed,"[3] Emma argues that "electronic research methods have become even more relevant for researchers in the context of the COVID-19 pandemic."[4] While virtual interviewing has traditionally

---

1. Elliston, *Missiological Research Design*, 7.
2. Dahlin, "Email Interviews," 1.
3. McHale, "Practical Guide," 1415.
4. Dahlin, "Email Interviews," 1.

received limited attention, post-COVID-19 has required researchers to adapt the methodology for remote data collection.[5]

The structured interview includes Burmese Buddhists, Myanmar liberal Christians, and Myanmar evangelical Christians. To address the research problem, the researcher adopted two methodologies, historical research and structured interview that typically study a relatively small number of individuals or situations.[6] In addition, the researcher sent the questionnaires to Buddhist monks, lay Buddhists, and contemporary Myanmar theologians to achieve the research goal.

The researcher examined the data from the interview about contemporary Burmese Nat worship and Myanmar Christianity. The structured interview was conducted after the dissertation committee approved the questions. In order to help the interviewees express and share their views, the researcher used structured interview questions. Interview questions were constructed to address the research questions thoroughly. The following research questions deserve attention to understand the pervasiveness of Nat worship in Myanmar.

Research Question 1: How is the Burmese primal religion (Nat Worship) so ubiquitous in Myanmar?

Operational Question 1.1: How prevalent is the Burmese Nat worship and Burmese Buddhism in their sociocultural and religiopolitical life?

Operational Question 1.2: How does the Burmese Nat worship inform everyday life among the Burmese Buddhists and Christians in Myanmar?

Operational Question 1.3: What is the impact of the Burmese Nat worship on the Christian churches in Myanmar?

Research question 1 and its subsequent operational questions aim at describing the pervasiveness of the Burmese Nat worship and its influence on the sociocultural and religiopolitical life of the people. The Burmese Buddhist-Nat worship makes up 87.9 percent of the country, whereas all other influences are far below that: 6.2 percent Christianity, 4.3 percent Islam, 0.8 percent Animists, 0.5 percent Hindus, 0.2 percent others, and none, 0.1 percent.[7] Therefore, this research question and the subsequent operational questions

---

5. Keen, Lomeli-Rodriguez, and Joffe. "Challenge to Opportunity," 1.
6. Bickman and Rog, *Applied Research Methods*, 75.
7. https://www.ethnologue.com/country/MM, accessed on 2 November 2022.

also aim to find out more about how the Burmese traditional religion informs their sociocultural and religiopolitical life.

In addition, research question 1 aims to discover how the Burmese traditional religion impacts their everyday life. Research question 1 is an important part of the study because it explores the prevalence of Burmese Buddhist-Nat worship in the society. It is important to understand Nat worship first and then approach it missiologically so that the mission of God would be grounded on the sociocultural and religiopolitical situation of the Burmese people and transform them into the kingdom of God.

Research Question 2: How does Nat worship contrast with a Trinitarian theology?

Operational Question 2:1: How does the concept of God in Nat worship contrast with Trinitarian worship?

Operational Question 2:2: How does the concept of salvation in Nat worship contrast with salvation in Christ alone?

Operational Question 2:3: How does the role of spirit in Nat worship contrast with the work of the Holy Spirit?

This study claims that the sociocultural and religiopolitical life of the Burmese is predominantly influenced by Buddhist-Nat worship, specifically the supernatural power of the Nat. Hence, the research question and its subsequent questions examine how Myanmar's society is receptive to a Trinitarian God because of its supernatural worldview. This research question and the operational questions are essential in determining how much the mission of God is anchored to the triune God and why the Burmese Nat worship principles have shaped Myanmar Christianity.

The Burmese Nat worship principles will be examined and compared in light of the Trinitarian *missio Dei* framework and the notion of suffering and salvation based on the redemptive work of Jesus Christ.

Research Question 3: What role does the church play in the context of Burmese Nat worship?

Operational Question 3:1: How can the Myanmar churches respond to those who became Christians but are going back to previous practices in order to meet their temporary need?

Operational Question 3:2: How can the mission of the church effectively engage with the mission field in the context of Burmese Nat worship?

Operational Question 3:3: How can the church address the need of the everyday life of Christians in the context of Burmese Nat worship?

Missiologists have done tremendous groundbreaking work on how the church responds to the challenge of ancestor worship, spirit worship, and indigenous religious practices. Research question 3 and its operational questions intend to explore the question of the conversion of the Burmese Nat worshipers through the proclamation of the gospel of Christ in the church. This research question will identify the significant meaning of conversion and discuss the dual allegiances of Burmese Nat and Christian beliefs, a syncretism of dual religious systems. In other words, some of these Christians go back to their previous practices whenever they meet daily problems such as illness, misfortune, drought, marriage, and failure in business.

This question traces some solutions for a missiological approach that seeks to transform the worldview of Nat worship to prevent these Christians with dual allegiances from returning to their previous religious rituals. The problem is that everyone has different worldviews, which can lead to different interpretations of the Scripture. Hence, it is important to recognize that our worldview is shaped by our upbringing, beliefs, and values that make sense of the world around us.[8]

Interview Findings

Interviews were conducted from July 2022–Sept 2022 via face-to-face and online platforms. The interviewees were Christians and Buddhists with different perspectives within their belief systems. There were thirteen participants in total, both face-to-face interviewees and online correspondents. There was evidence that some Buddhists embraced Nat worship as part of Buddhism, and others excluded Nat worship from Burmese Buddhism. In the same way, there was evidence that some Christian interviewees embraced that Buddhism and Nat worship enrich the Christian mission, while others excluded Nat worship and Buddhism because of syncretism.

A missiological approach to the relationship between the Burmese primal religion and Burmese Buddhism is to know what the Burmese primal religion and Burmese Buddhism have in common and what their relationship to

---

8. Rheenen, *Communicating Christ*, 95.

Christianity is. The present research sought to understand how the Burmese Buddhists individually and collectively understand the Burmese Nat worship and Buddhism. The researcher interviewed Buddhist monks, lay Buddhists, and contemporary Myanmar Christian theologians to obtain accurate data.

Research Approach

This researcher was only able to partially investigate the relationship between Burmese Nat worship, Buddhists, and Christianity. Due to the limitations of the scope of the research and the recent military coup, the present research was designed mainly to conduct historical and library research. The researcher studied Christian missionaries' literature in Myanmar.

Part of this study was focused on interviewing knowledgeable persons on Nat worship and Christian mission in Myanmar. The researcher initially obtained agreement with the interviewees via email, Viber, and Facebook; one refused but thirteen accepted. The researcher knew some of them from his previous work in Myanmar's Christian ministries and social services.

Recently, the researcher came to know about a Burmese Rakhine Buddhist monk by visiting the monastery in southside Indianapolis and interviewed him. The researcher's relatives and acquaintances were not interviewed. The criterion for selecting interviewees was limited to the accessibility of the person and his or her knowledge of the subject. The interviewees represented a wide range of ethnicity and religions. Buddhist monks and lay Buddhists from Rakhine, Burmese, and Kayah state, as well as contemporary liberal and evangelical Christians were interviewed.

It was a structured interview as the questions were prepared in advance and the same method was used during the interviews. Data were collected via email for the online interviews because the internet speed in Myanmar was not strong enough for a face-to-face interview. All the collected data were kept in a folder. The researcher analyzed the responses to the research questions and operational questions as the researcher used a structured interview for the data collection methods and had the transcript from those interviews.

To understand contemporary Burmese Nat worship and Buddhism as a religion, it is a good choice to use the phenomenological approach because the phenomenology of religion provides us with the inner structure and meaning of the essence of religion.[9] One of the reasons for the suitability of a phenomenological model is the setting aside of prejudgments and opening the research interview with unbiased, receptive presence.[10] Moreover, the phenomenological approach helps this study to categorize the elements of Burmese Nat worship and Burmese Buddhism such as objects, sacred space and times, and sacred actions. For example, Spiro discovered the ways – *aulan*, lower path and *atehlan*, upper path – of explaining suffering in a Burmese Nat-Buddhist context. According to Spiro's interviews, the *aulan*, lower path, witches cause illness and death and the *atehlan*, upper path witches cure illness but are not able to raise the dead.[11] Employing a phenomenological approach helps the researcher to discover ideas about local deity, evil spirits, eternal life, explanation for sufferings, and reconciliation.

The researcher read the interview data repeatedly to interpret and develop the various concepts and themes. The researcher approached the data with a qualitative method to look for ideas and concepts to establish a framework. Qualitative coding in this writing is a process of searching and identifying concepts and finding relations between Nat worship and Christianity in Myanmar. The interview was a one-time participation. There was no follow-up to get feedback from the interviewees because the questions were solely about concepts toward the primal religious practices of the people and the imported religions, Buddhism and Christianity. The researcher used a notebook to record the data and word documents for the online survey. Therefore, there was no pilot study to test the effectiveness of the interview questions.

Research Design

As aforementioned, the library research was done at the library of Concordia Theological Seminary in Fort Wayne, Indiana. Email correspondence and in-person interviews took place in Indianapolis. The researcher had made initial contact via phone calls and emails to the potential interviewees for the interview and the permission to use the material for the dissertation. The questionnaires for the interview were divided into two sections: one for the Christian

---

9. Plantinga, "Seeking Boundaries," 2.
10. Moustakes, *Phenomenological Research*, 180–82.
11. Spiro, *Burmese Supernaturalism*, 22.

theologians and the second for the Buddhists. Contemporary Christian theologians held various positions in theological seminaries and church ministries, whereas the Buddhist interviewees were monks and laypersons.

Table 1. The Interview Plans

July 2022–September 2022	Initial Plan	Realistic
Locations of research	Myanmar & USA	Yangon, Kalaymyo, and Chin State, USA, UK
Christian denominational background	Baptists	Baptist, Evangelical Baptist, Roman Catholic
Number of interview questions for Buddhists	8	8
Number of interview questions for Christians	10	10
Number of Buddhist interviewees	4	7
Number of Christian interviewees	3	6

The purpose of these interviews was to find out the daily practical experience of the people under the influence of Burmese Nat Buddhism and Christianity. The initial plan was to interview six people because of restricted access due to the military coup in Myanmar. However, the researcher was able to access thirteen people via face-to-face interview, and email to people living in Myanmar, the U.K., and the U.S. In addition, the researcher had access to Christian ministers in Myanmar who were teaching at different Theological Seminaries, pastoring in local churches, and working in non-profit organizations.

Interviews with people of Myanmar living in different parts of the world have enriched the study with different perspectives. For example, a Christian minister who was teaching at a seminary and another minister who was teaching at another seminary viewed the subject differently. In the same way, a Buddhist monk who was residing in the U.S. had different views from a lay Buddhist living in Myanmar. In other words, the views and geographical locations were relatively different for Buddhists and Christians.

Therefore, the interviewer was able to successfully capture why they believe what they believe – the researcher was able to interview six Christians and seven Buddhists. Interestingly, the researcher discovered different views on the relationship between Nat worship and Buddhism from the interviewees. For example, while some of the Buddhist interviewees accepted Nat worship to be part of Buddhism, others did not accept it. Similarly, while some Christian interviewees accepted elements of Nat worship and Buddhism that entails Christian missions, others did not because they viewed it as syncretism.

The researcher believes in the superiority of Christianity over other worldviews and religions; therefore, he identified as one who believes the Christian faith is the most complete religious system, which he tries to teach others in his professional life. Developing a relationship with the Burmese Buddhists in this research brings forth the opportunity to share the gospel with them.

Research Procedures

The Concordia Theological Seminary Fort Wayne required a research consent form signed between the interviewees and the researcher. The researcher conducted interviews face-to-face and via email after the dissertation committee screened and signed the consent form. The consent form plays a crucial role in guarding against any possible ethical problem. In addition, the dissertation committee reviewed the questionnaires drafted by the researcher to ensure that the research interview was conducted in such a way that it would not violate any culture or religion. In order to apply the ethical rules and consent form adopted by the researcher and the dissertation committee, the researcher obtained an initial agreement with the interviewees before the interview was carried out.

Before starting the interview, the researcher ensured that the participants read, understood, and signed the consent form. The interview was longer for those from Buddhist backgrounds, because it took a while to get to know and explain that the interview's purpose was only for the dissertation. The face-to-face interview lasted about forty to fifty minutes. The researcher recorded the interviews with notebooks. However, the online interviews via email were received in word document file. There were two sets of interview questions, one for Christians and another for Buddhists. The interview questions for Christians are given below.

1. Do you think Burmese Nat worship is prevalent in Myanmar?
2. In your understanding, what exactly is the Burmese traditional religion and its relationship to the sociocultural and religiopolitical life of the people?
3. In what areas do you think the Burmese Nat worship impacts on Buddhism and Christianity?
4. Do you think it is important to understand Burmese traditional practices to do the mission of God in the Burmese context?
5. Do you see the Burmese Nat worship principles as a barrier or an aid for Christian missions in Myanmar?
6. Do you agree that Burmese Nat-Buddhism influences Myanmar Christianity?
7. Do you think the concept of a triune God relates to the concept of supernaturalism in Burmese Nat worship?
8. What role do you think the Holy Spirit plays in the context of the Burmese Nat worship in Myanmar?
9. In your opinion, what is the most effective way to share salvation in the context of Nat worship?
10. What do you see as the role the church plays in Nat worship?

The interview questions for the Buddhists are given below.

1. How do you see Nat worship in Myanmar? Do you see that it tolerates Theravada Buddhism so that Burmese Nat worship exists side by side with Buddhism?
2. As a Buddhist, do you accept Nat worship as part of your religious practice?
3. If you see Nat worship and Buddhism as inseparable, in what ways do they adhere to one another?
4. As I grew up in Myanmar, I witnessed Buddhist businessmen performing prayer rituals on many occasions. For example, a driver invoked spirits by spraying ritual water on the bus so that the trip would be under the protection of spirits. Is this a practice of Buddhism or Nat worship or both?
5. Is there any misunderstanding between Buddhists and Nat worship?

6. Is there any similarity between Nat worship and Buddhism: for example, in terms of their relation to the socioeconomic and religiopolitical life of the people?
7. Is there any difference between Nat worship and Buddhism regarding life after death?
8. Do you see any similarity between Burmese Nat worship and Christianity?

The researcher initiated the process by filling out the consent form, and having the interviewee fill out the consent form by himself or herself. The researcher assured the interviewees that his or her religion would not be criticized. Sure enough, one of the interviewees told the researcher to not criticize other faiths in the interview process. However, throughout the interviews, there were no ethical or religious issues.

CHAPTER 4

Research Findings and Analysis

Among the thirteen participants in the structured interview, four were from the U.S., one from the U.K., and the rest from Myanmar. Two participants were interviewed in a face-to-face interview and the others were via the online platform. This section emphasizes the research findings from the research interviews and the historical research at the school library. The researcher repeatedly mentioned that the interviewees' identities would be kept confidential. The interviews for this research were voluntary as the individuals received no money in order to complete the interview. The average face-to-face interview lasted from forty to sixty minutes, and those who responded via email took about one month to complete and send the interview responses back to the researcher.

The researcher employed a deductive coding approach as the codes are developed based on the research questions, framework, and literature reviews.[1] The purpose of coding in this research is not only generating themes, concepts, and ideas, but also labeling and assigning certain parts of the text to organize it. But Saldana states that coding is not just labeling; it is *linking*.[2] In addition, the researcher previously applied data analysis and qualitative coding as he worked for the Action Contre la Faim [INGO] in Myanmar.[3] Similarly, Saldana sets out several ways or functions of coding.

---

1. Emma, "Qualitative Coding." See also, Wiley, "DMS975–Missiological Research Design."

2. Saldana, *Coding Manual*, 8.

3. The researcher worked as a Liaison Officer for Action Contre la Faim France-Based for Myanmar Mission from 2008–2011.

For example, Saldana asserts, Ms. B is used as a code given to Ian's friend.[4] A codebook explains all the concepts and variables present in the data files including numerical values, range, and scheme classification. Understanding the way of qualitative coding helps us understand the table below. For example, CM50 applied to C in the table as Christian, M as Male, 50 as age, and B as Buddhist, F as Female, and 43 as age.

Table 2. Interview Participant Demographic Overview

Participants in order	Age	Gender	Location	Method of Interview	Code
Interviewee #1	50	M	Myanmar	Email	CM50
Interviewee #2	43	F	Myanmar	Email	BF43
Interviewee #3	34	F	Georgia, US	Email	BF34
Interviewee #4	40	M	Indiana, US	Face-to-face	BM40
Interviewee #5	26	F	Indiana, US	Face-to-face	BF26
Interviewee #6	56	F	Myanmar	Email	CM56
Interviewee #7	42	M	Myanmar	Email	CM42-1
Interviewee #8	42	M	Myanmar	Email	CM42-2
Interviewee #9	46	M	Myanmar	Email	CM46
Interviewee #10	33	F	UK	Email	BF33
Interviewee #11	63	F	Myanmar	Email	BF63
Interviewee #12	37	F	Myanmar	Email	BF37
Interviewee #13	45	M	Kentucky	Email	CM45

Every participant was given a consent form to notify them about the nature of the research and possible outcome. Two face-to-face interviews were conducted at a Coffee House at Southport Road, Indianapolis. This location was chosen because it is a quiet environment conducive for interviews. All other interviews were conducted via email. The researcher was able to record every single interview in word document files.

---

4. Saldana, *Coding Manual*, 27.

Interview Responses

Question 1. How do you see Nat Worship in Myanmar? Do you see that it tolerates Theravada Buddhism so that Burmese Nat worship exists side by side with Buddhism?

Participant BF34 responded, "I personally think that Nat worship is traditional Buddhism." While Nat worship is a traditional animistic practice that involves the worship of spirits or deities, Buddhism is a religion that is based on the teaching of the Buddha. From the standpoint of interview participants, there is a cultural and historical connection. The first question is the leading question that guides the respondents toward understanding Burmese Nat worship and Theravada Buddhism. The researcher started with this question to elicit responses confirming their preconceived notions of the following questions.

After screening the survey data, all seven Buddhist interviewees agreed that Nat worship and Buddhism do not share anything in common. Notwithstanding this, they hesitated to separate one from the other. From the research findings, the difference between Nat and Buddhism could be confirmed by the reoccurring phrases and themes in the interview. Most participants repeatedly mentioned that Nat worship was a traditional religion before Gautama became the Buddha; however, pure Theravada Buddhists do not worship Nat while popular Buddhists do.

One thing all the participants agreed to is that the Buddha taught humans to do good deeds to all living things, including to the Nat. Participant BM40 conceived that Nat worship tolerates Theravada Buddhism. Participant BF63 was of the opinion that Nat worship had no problem with Buddhism. Conversely, Burmese Buddhism had a little problem with the government because the Burmese Buddhist government officials used Nat rituals to overcome the opponents' political parties. In the same vein, participant BF26 states that Nat worship is very different from Buddhism, at the same time, confessing that she placed a Nat shrine side by side with the Buddha image at home. Participant BF33 states that Nat worship in Myanmar is not related to religion but it is more of a traditional practice that tolerates Buddhism in order to coexist. Participant BF37 states that "Nat tolerates Buddhism in many ways. For example, there are the anointed and virtuous Nat that entitled monks to homage, but there are lower Nat who are not deserving of homage." Participant BF43 responds that "feeding meat to Nat does not mean worshiping but just good deeds. As a Buddhist, there is nothing wrong with offering meat to Nat because it is counted as good deeds."

The preceding paragraph stated that all the participants interviewed had at least one similar concept in common, that is, good deeds are a path to nirvana. However, they have different views on other aspects such as Nat worship as a religion or a traditional practice. Participant BF43 believed that feeding raw meat to Nat is part of Burmese Buddhist practice as a way of doing a good deed, not necessarily the act of worship. The findings from the interview question 1 suggest that Nat worship and Buddhism are deeply interwoven in the belief and practical life of the interviewees. The answers given by interview participants for the first structured interview question were well aligned with the research question and operational questions. All seven Buddhists interview participants expressed that though Nat worship and Buddhism are not inherently linked, Burmese people have incorporated them into their daily life.

Question 2. As a Buddhist, do you accept Nat worship to be part of your religious practice? This is a part of question 1. How they view the toleration of Nat worship determined the level of relationship Nat had with Buddhism. Participant BF63 said that "Nat worship is not a religious practice. However, it is part of the family's cultural tradition on the father's side for the male of the family is obliged to carry on the practice of honoring two kinds of Nat." For participant BF63, Buddhism is her religion and Nat worship is her cultural practice. The challenge here is how to distinguish religion from culture. Participants BF34, BF26, BF33, and BF43 considered Nat worship as not part of their religious practice. However, they all agreed to wish for goodwill toward Nat because it accumulates merits to break the cycle of life. For participant BF63, Nat worship is a cultural practice that has nothing to do with religion, however, participants BF34, BF26, BF33, and BF43 viewed Nat worship as helping them to break the cycle of life to attain nirvana.

The interview participants understood the questions and could provide accurate and relevant responses that validated the research questions' findings by addressing the influence of Nat on human affairs and bring good and bad fortune. For example, participant BF26 stated, "Nat is fed with raw meat as to please [sic] which is not worship in a deep sense of the term worship." Participant BM40 responded, "In order to avoid such naturally disastrous events, Buddhists wish goodwill toward Nat." Participants BF34, BF43, and

BF63 gave the same views that Nat worship is deeply ingrained in the belief system, customs, and traditions of the Burmese people. This is vividly seen in the way Burmese military leaders have used Nat worship as a tool for political power and influence in Burmese society.

From a Christian point of view, Nat worshipers could be Buddhists at the same time because they accepted fragments of Nat worship to benefit Buddhists. Myanmar today is one of the most devoutly Buddhist countries in the world and anybody who is perceived to have insulted Buddhism, intentionally or not, could face jail. Interestingly, however, Burmese Buddhism actually has a strong tradition of Nat worship as part of their religion. As most of the participants interviewed stated, Nat worship is not a formal religion, it tolerated Buddhism and became part of Buddhism.

Out of seven participants only participant BF26, who said "feeding meat to Nat is not worshiping," boldly stated that "a pure and true Buddhist would not invoke spirits in order to protect the journey." Participant BF43 mentioned, "the Buddha once said there are no such things as I must worship my god alone," which means one can worship many gods, so the Buddha himself allowed others to tolerate his teachings. Participant BF43's responses suggest that the Burmese Buddhists can worship more than one god, aligning with contemporary liberal Christians in Myanmar. For example, a liberal Christian in Myanmar had once preached that Buddhists and Christians go different ways, but they reach the same destination.

Question 3. If you see Nat worship and Buddhism as inseparable, in what way do they adhere to one another? The preceding three questions are clustered with each other. In other words, they are connected so that the answer to question 3 is already hinted at in the previous responses. According to participant BM40, Burmese Buddhists cannot avoid Nat worship especially when disasters such as cyclones, landside, and sickness occur. Burmese Buddhists believe that when Nat is angry with human beings, resulting sickness, misfortune, and natural disasters happen. Therefore, the Burmese Buddhists make offerings to propitiate them. Participant BF34 stated that "Nat worship and Burmese Buddhism are inseparable." For example, there are many Nat shrines in Buddhist pagodas in Myanmar. Participants BF43 and BF37 agreed that popular Buddhists have compromised with Nat worship. In other words, the question is how to differentiate between pure Theravada Buddhism and popular Buddhism.

Until question 3, the phrases, "a true Buddhist," and "a popular Buddhist," frequently reoccurred to describe people who perceived Buddhism as a religion or a cultural practice. It is difficult for a Burmese Buddhist to ban Nat worship. Nevertheless, the interesting question is, why is it so? Indeed, every Myanmar citizen knows where to look for the signs of Nat worship as they are everywhere. Examples are a white-and-red cloth tied to a car's rear-view mirror or a small shrine under a tree. When King Anawratha came to power in the eleventh century, he abandoned Nat worship and ordered the destruction of all shrines in public places, the people brought Nat shrines home. Today you will find Nat shrines alongside every typical Burmese home.

Question 4. As I grew up in Myanmar, I was an eyewitness of Buddhist businessmen performing prayer rituals on many occasions. For example, a driver invoked spirits by spraying ritual water on the bus so that the trip would be under the protection of spirits. Is this practice Buddhism or Nat worship or both?

Participants BM40, BF34, and BF63, stated "that invoking Nat or spirits is common in Buddhism." However, there are various reasons for that. For example, participant BM40 asserted "that it is a normal Buddhist practice," whereas participant BF34 believed that a Buddhist driver recites the Buddhist scripture to chase away evil spirits. Participant BF34 responded to operational research question 2, the concept of suffering and explanation in Burmese Nat worship. As mentioned in the literature review, suffering in Nat worship is often attributed to the wrath of Nat. As a result, Nat worshipers perform rituals or offer sacrifices to appease them and seek their blessings for protection and well-being.

However, participant BF63 agreed that such practice is found in both Nat worship and Buddhism, because a Nat or a monk blessed the ritual water while reciting a *paritta* sermon, which is believed to offer protection against evil spirits in their journey. Participant BF33 suggested that this is simply Nat worship because it is found among non-Buddhists who follow such ritual practices. Buddhism viewed such spirits as low mortals – subject to death or can die – who need help from human beings. One of the recurring themes in the survey was "pure Buddhist."

There may be some parallels that could be drawn between Nat worship and the concept of suffering and salvation in Christianity. For example, in both cases, suffering is seen as a part of the human condition, and people seek redemption from it. However, it is important to note from the responses in the structured interview and literature that there are significant differences between Nat worship and Christianity, including the beliefs about the nature of suffering, the concept of salvation, and the role of divine beings or forces. Hence, Christians believe that Jesus, as the Son of God, willingly suffered and died on the cross to redeem humanity from sin and offer salvation.

It is important to note that the ritual water, an element of Nat worship, vividly surfaced in the structured interview. Simon Pau Khan En stated that elements of Nat worship enrich the Christian mission in Myanmar. For example, ritual water is one of the elements Burmese Nat-Buddhists often use in ceremonies, festivals, and ritual practices. Every Burmese Buddhist household places clean water in a container on an elevated surface, such as an altar or dedicated Nat worship area. It is a prayer or expression of gratitude to the Nat as appreciation for their blessings. Therefore, employing elements of Nat worship is idolatry and not aligned with a traditional Christian mission.

Question 5. Is there any misunderstanding between Buddhists and Nat worship? Rather than misunderstanding, participants BF33 and BF43 stated that "there is confusion between the two faiths." One participant asserted that Nat worship is a big setback to attaining nirvana for Buddhists. Participant BF43 explained that there is no misunderstanding between Buddhists and Nat worship because the Buddha taught human beings that one must not worship one god alone. Moreover, there is no wrong belief or worship because when one contends that one's religion is the best, this is considered self-centered and the path to suffering. Participant BM40 asserted that there is no misunderstanding between Buddhists and Nat worship because the Burmese Buddhists believe there are spirits who control designated areas. Participant BF37 responded with a particular concept of why the Burmese Nat worship and Buddhism do not misunderstand each other. Far be it from a misunderstanding between Nat worship and Buddhism, according to BF37. Rather, virtuous and integral Nat follow the teaching of the Buddha, Dharma, and Sangha. Therefore, it is wrong to worship Nat who is not virtuous and not attached to the teaching of the Buddha.

According to participant BF37, Nat worship and Buddhism have merged very well, although there are different practices. She added that some Nat do not benefit human beings because they are not virtuous Nat as they do not follow the teaching of the Buddha. In this sense, Nat and Buddhism are inseparable. Participant BF63 pointed out that Theravada Buddhists recognize celestial beings also known as Nat, who had been reborn in the heavens due to good merits while some Nat were lower beings and guardians of trees; but Buddhists do not worship either group. Interestingly, participant BF33 thought Buddhism is not about worship, rather it offers guidance that allows one to test and challenge. On the one hand, a Buddhist does not believe in someone else, but that you reap what you sow. On the other hand, Nat worship heavily relies on ritual and sacrificial offerings out of fear and for reward.

In the same vein, liberal Christians in Myanmar insist on interfaith dialogue between Buddhists and Christians to reduce misunderstandings, misconceptions, and prejudices, and promote peaceful coexistence and cooperation among diverse religious communities. However, Christianity and Buddhism are distinct religious traditions with different ends or ultimate goals. The ultimate goal of authentic Christian belief is eternal peace, whereas liberal Christians are concerned more about social justice and cohesion, stability, and peacebuilding in their society. The structured interview and historical research shed light on the different beliefs and practices, and that liberalists misinterpret the divine role Christ plays in his redemptive work.

Question 6. Is there any similarity between Nat worship and Buddhism: for example, concerning the socioeconomic and religiopolitical life of the people?

Structured interview question 6 simultaneously responds to question 2 of the Christian interviews which is about the socioeconomic life of the people. Participant BM40 said that "there are similarities between Nat worship and Buddhism's socioeconomic and religiopolitical concerns." According to BM40, Nat worship and Buddhism viewed socioeconomic and religiopolitical concerns as two sides of the same coin. A liberal Christian theologian encourages Myanmar churches to engage in various forms of poverty alleviation efforts. Churches can play a role in providing social economic development for alleviating poverty, but the primary teaching of the church is lost when the church focuses on equality between the gospel and socioeconomic life. However, participant BF26 disagreed that there are similarities between Nat worship and Buddhism in every detailed aspect. For example, while Nat worship emphasizes short-term, Buddhism emphasizes long-term vision in life. The former is about passing one's exams this year and the latter is focused on reaching nirvana. As a result, Nat worship has only a temporary vision.

Participants CM42-1, CM42-2, CM50, and CM45 stated the "socioeconomic life of the Burmese people [is] deeply intertwined with Nat worship and Buddhism." For example, participant CM45 pointed out that "to be Buddhist is to be Burmese and vice-versa." According to participants BF34 and BF33, "Nat worship and Buddhism are intermingled in their socioeconomic and religiopolitical life." However, participant BF33 asserted that popular Buddhists back up their political aims with their socioeconomic concern. Participant BF63 said that both Nat worship and Buddhism each practice their beliefs in different ways. For example, Nat worshipers appease Nat for fortune, prosperity, health, and good weather. On the other hand, Burmese Buddhists perform good deeds to attain nirvana. In other words, Buddhists prioritize nirvana over fortune, prosperity, health and good weather. Nat worshipers are concerned with terrestrial things whereas Buddhists are concerned with celestial things.

Question 7. Is there any difference between Nat worship and Buddhism in terms of life after death?

Participant BF34, a Buddhist, believed in the next life and reincarnation. Participant BF26 believed that there is a difference between Nat worship and Buddhism about life after death. Nat worshipers go straight to hell, but a Buddhist who utters a genuine prayer before his or her death may attain nirvana. The question remains as to whom do Buddhists pray. Participant BF33 believed that there is no life after death in Nat worship, whereas, in Buddhism, there is life after death according to karmic law. Participant BF63 stated that Nat, as a spirit being, exists in life after death. Buddhism denies the existence of an unchanging soul that transmigrates from this life to the next. In this perspective, there is a striking difference in belief concerning life after death between Nat worship and Buddhism.

Question 7 is a fundamental question. As Lennox convincingly suggests, "Every one of us needs a worldview to construct our belief system,"[5] the Burmese worldview, which is based on Nat worship, shapes their belief systems. Interestingly, as mentioned in Chapter 2, the Burmese belief system, Nat worship, shapes their worldview rather than the worldview shaping their beliefs. Buddhism does not believe in a permanent, unchanging soul that persists after death; it teaches the concept of rebirth or reincarnation as there

---

5. Gooding and Lennox, *Questioning Our Knowledge*, 3.

is no such thing as death but flight to Nibban, liberation from suffering that is to attain enlightenment. On the one hand, the missiological message of Christianity is salvation through faith in Christ to receive but not earn eternal life.

Question 8. Do you see any similarity between Burmese Nat worship and Christianity?

Participant BF26 asserted that the difference between Nat worship and Christianity lies in humans' final destination. Participant BF33 believed that the similarity between Nat worship and Christianity is their practice of worship. Unlike Buddhists, Christians believe in the creator God. Similarly, Nat worshipers believe in creation that is protected by spirits. Participant BF34 believed that the similarity between Nat worship and Christianity is that they both believe in the existence of God but there are many Nat or gods in Nat worship. All participants acknowledged their limited knowledge of Christianity and, hesitated to respond to question 8. However, their basic understanding of Christianity sums up what Christianity is all about. Christianity is about human final destination, worship, and Creator. Question 8 is appropriate for both Buddhist and Christian interview participants. All the Burmese Buddhist interview participants had limited knowledge for two reasons: Christianity is a minority religion, and the two religions have distinct beliefs, practices, and histories. However, participant BF34 thought that "Christians believe there is only one God, whereas there are many deities in Nat worship." Participant BF33 stated, "Based on my understanding, the similarity would be the concept of worshiping."

Although Buddhist interview participants expressed the different belief systems between Burmese Nat-Buddhism and Christianity, liberal Christians in Myanmar insisted on drawing elements from Nat worship to Christian mission. Therefore, the first American Protestant missionary to Myanmar constantly preached the Christian God as a triune God, the Father, Son, and Holy Spirit, to distinguish the Christian God from other gods. For example, a Christian interview participant (CM42-1) responded that the concept of a supernatural being in animistic belief sheds light on the concept of the Trinity in Christianity. That eased Christians' approach to the context of Nat worship. However, the mission of God rooted in a Trinitarian *missio Dei* distances the Christian mission from compromising with local deities.

Online Responses for Nat Worship and Christianity.

Question 1. How do you see the relationship between Burmese Nat worship and Theravada Buddhism in Myanmar, and how it impacts Christian mission?

Participant CM46 stated that "Myanmar Nat worship had been practiced since time immemorial." Therefore, Nat worship is the first religion in Myanmar. When King Anawratha came to power in AD 1044, he invaded the Mon region and captured a famous Buddhist monk, Shin Arahan. The monk converted the king to Theravada Buddhism, and they abandoned Nat worship by destroying Nat shrines across the country.

Participant CM45 agreed with participant CM46 that the abolition of Nat worship failed because the Nat shrines, which were destroyed in the forest, were brought home. All Christian participants in the online interview agreed that Nat tolerated Buddhism and then Buddhism impacted Christianity. However, participant CM45 stated that "the relationship between Nat worship and Buddhism does not have any impact on Evangelical Christian missions," and was optimistic that it has impacts, however, on Christian missions through the inter-faith and ecumenical missions. On the other hand, participant CM46 said, "It is extremely important to understand Burmese traditional practices [Nat worship] in order to do the mission of God in Burmese context because Christianity came into Myanmar along with colonialism." The impact of Nat worship on Christianity necessitates rooting the gospel of Christ in the soil of Myanmar.

According to data collection from all Buddhist and Christian participants interviewed, Nat worship has established a long-standing relationship with Christianity, which has, over time, significantly impacted Christian beliefs and practices in Myanmar. From this perspective, Burmese Christians are split into two different groups. Some Christians employ inter-faith dialogue as a missiological approach, and others insist on proclaiming the gospel as a missiological approach to the Burmese Buddhists.

Question 2. In your understanding, what exactly is the Burmese traditional religion and its relationship to the sociocultural and religiopolitical life of the people?

When it comes to the relationship between socioeconomic and religiopolitical life in Myanmar, it is a puzzling paradox. On the one hand, the Burmese government officials claimed Theravada Buddhism as their state religion, which encouraged generosity and nonviolence, but they did not follow its teaching. On the other hand, Theravada Buddhism is known for its nonviolent movement, but the Myanmar junta and their followers are the most violent soldiers who massacre thousands of their people.

Participants CM42-1, CM42-2, and CM50 stated that Animism significantly influenced Buddhism as well as their socioeconomic and political life. One way to describe its influence is the annual festival Buddhists hold to offer enormous things to Nat, so that Nat in turn will bestow blessings the following year. However, participant CF56 provokingly stated that many Buddhists are confused in their faith since the military coup on 1 February 2022, which started a nationwide political and economic crisis. According to her, while the military junta leaders seemed to follow the teaching of conservative Buddhist monks, they secretly practiced astrology and horoscope. Participant CM50 asserted that Burmese Buddhist families invited jungle spirits by offering a sacrificial animal to solve their daily problems. For example, if a family member gets sick, the parents invite *Natkadaw* – a female spirit – to heal the sick person. Participant CM46 stated that "Burmese Buddhism is the backbone of the sociocultural and political life of the people." Participant CM45 viewed socioeconomic concerns and Burmese Buddhism as deeply interwoven and inseparable.

The responses from all Christian interview participants simultaneously answer research question 1 and its operational questions. Examining the evidence through a Trinitarian *missio Dei* lens and with a Christocentric and ecclesio-centric focus based on Scripture shed light on how liberal Christians in Myanmar perceive the need for interfaith dialogue and the mission of God in the context of encounters between Burmese Buddhist-Nat worship and Christianity. A Christian interview participant (CF56) stated, "Currently, various people groups in Myanmar are passing through a nationwide political and economic crisis since the military coup (Feb 2021). Most of them are experiencing the great depression and their responses to these political, economic and social situations are complex."

Question 3. In what areas do you think the Burmese Nat worship impact Buddhism and Christianity?

Participant CM42-1 had witnessed the impact of Burmese Nat worship on both Buddhism and Christianity. For example, he said, "Nat worship plays a significant role for Buddhists in deciding the date for the wedding, naming a child, and palmistry." Many proclaimed Christians were secretly attached to their old ways of thought so they would go to the gravesite of their loved ones bringing for them food, drink, and cloth to get advice for life. Participant CM42-2 thought Nat worship impacted Buddhism and Christianity in terms of healing and bringing luck for prosperity.

Participant CF56 responded that the impact of Nat worship on Christianity was seen in the belief in dreams. "The Burmese Buddhist converts continued to believe in astrology, horoscope, and palm reading in order to be delivered from the bondage of sickness, poverty, and misfortune." Participants CM42-1 and CF56 viewed the impact of Nat worship on Christianity in the same way. Participant CM50 however, believed that, in rural areas a Christian child could be crying for no known cause and so the child is believed to be disturbed by ancestors. It is believed that disrespect to an ancestor causes the event, and offering is demanded to heal such illness.

The above interview responses demonstrated that the impact of Nat worship and Buddhism on Christianity is visible as some Christians blended the two belief systems, Nat worship and Christianity. For example, when Christians have temporary problems, they go back to previous practices such as astrology, horoscope, and palm reading to solve their daily crisis. The problems Christians face in a religiously pluralistic society are related to dealing with their religious past – prayers, rituals, songs, and spiritual exorcism. According to the researcher, there are two problems: First, when people converted to the Christian faith, the missionary and native pastor often removed elements attached to their cultural practices such as drum, gong, flute, alcoholic drink, and food, because these are considered unbiblical. It left a cultural vacuum that needed to be filled. Too often, the foreign-trained pastors and missionaries replaced them by importing customs, which were foreign to the native people.

In light of the interview participants, it is crucial to approach Nat worship with spirit exorcism as part of their spiritual practices, with the aim to drive out evil spirits and restoring spiritual well-being. Of course, there may be different theological interpretations and perspectives on the nature of evil spirits, possession, and the appropriate use of exorcism within Christian traditions. But exorcism is appropriate to apply this in the context of Burmese Nat worship.

The second problem is when a Christian intermarries with a person from other religions such as Buddhism and Islam, a formal Christian wedding is held in the church and then another wedding ceremony in the monastery or mosque. The question remains, who makes the right decision in this kind of situation? In all these situations we hold that, the primary source for understanding the mission of God in a pluralistic context is the word of God.

Question 4. Do you think it is important to understand Burmese traditional practices in order to do the mission of God in the Burmese context? Participant CM42-1 responded that "context [is] very important in interpreting and preaching biblical messages." Thus, we need to understand the Burmese traditional practices for effectively doing the mission of God among the Burmese people. The participant is optimistic about the effectiveness of the mission of God only if the word of God is interpreted adequately in the context. Participants CM42-2, CF56, CM46, and CM45 agree with participant CM42-1 on the importance of understanding the context in doing the mission of God. However, participant CM42-1 pointed out that it is necessary to interpret the word of God adequately whereas participant CM46 thought that because colonialism came along with Christianity, understanding the context is crucial in doing Christian mission.

Participant CM45 asserted that understanding the context may help the effectiveness of Christian missions, but one may need to study where the context is. According to participant CM45, the city and rural village have different cultural contexts. Therefore, context plays a crucial role in the effectiveness of mission communication. Interview question 4 is the backbone of the study and it vividly responded to the research question 3 and its operational questions, which is the mission of God in the context of Burmese Nat worship. Therefore, it is essential to carry out the mission of God with humility, respect, and a deep understanding of the local culture and beliefs. Therefore the ultimate goal should be preaching the gospel for the conversion of the people.

Therefore, the researcher investigates the importance of mission communication for God's mission, especially in the pluralistic country of Myanmar. There are two approaches accordingly. First, French philosopher Jacques Derrida influences a postmodern view of mission communication, which stresses the reconstruction or deconstruction of the word of God. The problem with a postmodern view of mission communication is that the same word in one context may have radically different meanings in another context. Interpreting the gospel in another context is key to the effectiveness of the mission of God. The translator's opinion can change the meaning of the message of God. Missionaries and pastors should allow the written word of God to direct one's life in confession, commitment, and repentance. In other words, the Word, Logos, is the primary principle of understanding the created thing, and therefore, God cannot be apprehended without the Logos, *Nisi per Verbum*.[6]

Adoniram Judson's approach is aligned with the Lutheran view of translation. It has been said that "Mr. Judson's Bible is to the Burmese people what Luther's Bible is to the German and the King James Version to the English-speaking races."[7] Translating the name of God in indigenous languages is a daunting task. For that reason, Judson acquired an excellent knowledge of the Burmese language and Pali, by which the sacred text of Buddhism was written. Therefore, Judson translated the name of God into Burmese, *thavara phaya*, to include the concept of a triune God and to distinguish it from national deities.[8]

Question 5. Do you see Burmese Nat worship principles as a barrier or an aid for Christian mission in Myanmar?

Participant MC42-1 responded that Nat worship could be both an aid and a barrier, but emphasized that one must not compromise Nat worship with the gospel. He added that the power of the gospel does not match with that of Nat. In contrast, participant CM42-2 thought that Nat worship principles might not be an aid for Christian missions in Myanmar. He noted that Nat worship could be a barrier rather than a bearer for the gospel of Christ in Myanmar.

Participant CF56 carefully observed that some principles of Nat worship could be barriers while others, similar to biblical tradition, could be aids for mission among Burmese Buddhists. Interestingly, she observed that biblical tradition shared similarities with Nat worship in terms of principles. What similar principles from Nat worship become aids for Christian missions has yet to unfold. Participants CM45 and CM46 noted that syncretism is not a barrier to Christian mission in the pluralistic society of Myanmar. However, the level of syncretism that the participants CM45 and CM46 referred to is still different. For example, participant CM45 was concerned that syncretism and contextualization should be distinct. In contrast, participant CM46

---

6. Gadamer, *Truth and Method*, 406.
7. Hubbard, *Ann of Ava*, 232.
8. Bailey, *Adoniram Judson*, 61.

viewed religious syncretism as necessary for rooting the gospel of Christ in the soil of pluralistic nations.

A difficult question is how one should relate with and simultaneously witness to people of other faiths without compromising. It is one of the most crucial missiological questions facing Christians in the twenty-first century. Hence, the communication of the Christians to a non-Christian community needs to be crystal clear without compromising with any other faith. Instead of the social context, the word of God should play a vital role in constituting the meaning of the gospel.

Although participants CM45 and CM46 thought that syncretism is not a barrier to the Christian mission, the researcher believes that syncretism might diminish the Christian faith in many ways. A practical example is whenever syncretistic Christians face problems, they consult astrology and witchcraft to solve their daily crisis such as health and misfortune. Judson knew that consulting astrologers and horoscopes in Myanmar defected the Christian faith, therefore, he never encouraged new converts to go back to previous practices. The interview participants simultaneously responded to previous questions, especially the elements of Nat worship in Christian missions. For example, one of the elements of Nat worship previously mentioned was ritual water. The researcher concisely argues that the element of Nat worship, ritual water, deliberately hinders the growth and flourishing of Christianity in Myanmar.

Question 6. Do you agree that Burmese Nat-Buddhism influences Myanmar Christianity? If yes, in what way or if not, why?

Participant CM42-1 thought that Burmese Nat-Buddhism influences the lives of Christians in Myanmar regarding decision-making, social life, and thoughts. In contrast, participant CM42-2 did not see the influences of Nat-Buddhism on Christianity because Christians go to church every Sunday. Participant CM50 suggested that Burmese Nat-Buddhism influences more poor and nominal Christians than faithful Christians. However, participant CF56 disagreed with the interview questions above that Burmese Nat-Buddhism does not influence Christianity because traditional Christians are more committed to missionary work than making dialogue with Burmese Nat-Buddhism.

Burmese Nat worship and Buddhism influence human affairs as they believe that Nat can bring luck and prosperity to those who appease and worship them, but at the same time, Nat can bring danger and misfortune to those who do not respect them. Nominal Christians in Myanmar tend to observe certain rules of Nat worship. For example, the researcher visited Loikaw city, Kayah State of Myanmar, in 2004, and a Burmese Nat-Buddhist told him to avoid wearing a black shirt because the guardian Nat of the city did not like it. Whether out of fear or simply to comply, the researcher changed into a different shirt.

The influence of Nat worship on Christians seems limited, as the majority of the population practices Buddhism. But one might be wrong to assume that statement as Nat worship still largely influences even Christians in those communities, particularly in making a decision such as a date for a wedding ceremony, palm reading, and taking food and drink to the cemetery of ancestors to ask for advice.

Question 7. Do you think the concept of a triune God relates to the concept of supernaturalism in Burmese Nat worship?

Participants CM42-1, CM42-2, CM50, and CM46 stated that the Chin, Kachin, Karen, Shan, Mon, and Rakhine ethnic groups have the concept of a supernatural being which relates to a triune God. In contrast, participant CF56 thought that the concept of a triune God relates to traditional Buddhism rather than Nat worship. However, she indicated that the concept of supernaturalism relates to Pentecostal-Charismatic spirituality. Although all participants viewed the concept of a triune God as relating to a supernatural being, no participants suggested the approach and method one should take in teaching about the triune God. Participant CF56 viewed that there is a certain degree to which the concept of a Trinitarian God relates to Burmese Buddhism.

A triune theology of mission is crucial in the Christian mission because "the *missio spiritus* is the one side of the coin of which the other is the *missio trinitatis*, meaning that any further understanding of the work of the divine wind in mission enables deeper comprehension of the redemptive witness of the triune Father, Son, and Spirit to save the world."[9] As Apostle Paul warned the Corinthians, "For such are false apostles, deceitful workers, transforming themselves into apostles of Christ. For Satan himself transforms himself into an angel of light" (2 Cor 11:13–14). It is crucial to test whether the spirit is

---

9. Yong, *Mission After Pentecost*, 14.

from God or Satan. The Spirit of God is inseparable from the Father and the Son in all activities. Without the Father sending his Son and the Father and Son sending the Holy Spirit into the world, there is no salvation because salvation history involves the activity of the triune God. The mission of God is incomplete, and one cannot discuss the Christian mission without Jesus Christ, the Son who was incarnated, died, and was resurrected, and the Holy Spirit, who dwells in Christians.[10]

Question 8. What role do you think the Holy Spirit plays in the context of the Burmese Nat worship in Myanmar?

Participant CM42-1 believed that "the Holy Spirit plays a significant role in proclaiming the Gospel of Jesus Christ to the Nat worshipers. Since Nat is a spirit being, the Holy Spirit encounters demonic spirits in the mission of God." Therefore, the Christian mission is a powerful counter ministry. Participant CM42-2 stated that the Holy Spirit plays the role of a good spirit or god in Myanmar and therefore, at any rate, spirit became an important point of contact for the mission of God. The Holy Spirit, the third person of the Trinity, is central to Christian theology of mission.

The power of the Holy Spirit in Christian missions enables Christians to witness boldly and effectively as it demonstrates God's love and compassion, and transforms individuals and communities. In addition, the Holy Spirit provides guidance, discernment, and empowerment to Christians as they engage in various forms of mission work, such as preaching and teaching the word of God. Therefore, the power of the Holy Spirit is essential in fulfilling the Great Commission, which is the mandate given by Jesus to his followers to make disciples of all nations (Matt 28:19–20).

Participant CF56 suggested that God created everything, seen and unseen, through his Word and Spirit. Moreover, the Holy Spirit is close to the poor, the needy, and marginalized people. She contended that whether one believed it or not, the Christian God is the creator of the universe and everything in it. Participant CM46 noted that Nat worship plays the role of *preparatio evangelica* for Burmese Nat worshipers and the ethnic indigenous people in Myanmar.

The role of the Holy Spirit is very powerful in the Christian mission. Dr. Schulz persuasively asserts, "When God comes to man, the Holy Spirit can

---

10. Schulz, *Mission from the Cross*, 91.

also seize the heart as the innermost seat of man's spirituality and instill very explicit emotions such as joy and peace."[11] On the one hand, the concept of spirits existing could be a point of contact with the Nat worship; on the other hand, it is a power encounter between evil spirits and the Holy Spirit. Therefore, spiritual exorcism is the only answer for any problem in the Nat worship context. In his book, titled *I Am Nat Afraid: Demon Possession and Spiritual Warfare*, Dr. Robert Bennett warns that, "Because of the continued mixing of false religious beliefs with Christianity (syncretism) the Malagasy Church trusts the *Fifohazana* movement to deal with spirit-possession not only among the heathen, but also with its own members."[12] As a result, a Trinitarian *missio Dei* increasingly becomes an important driving force in the Christian mission, especially in the context of spirit worship.

Question 9. In your opinion what is the most effective way to share salvation in the context of Nat worship?

Participant CM42-1 believed that the most effective way to proclaim the gospel in the context of Nat worship is power encounters such as performing miraculous healing and casting out demons. It is the most effective way because the people of Myanmar worship Nat out of fear rather than love. Participant CM42-1 believed that people will worship God if there were a more powerful spirit than Nat who could deliver them from the bondage of fear, sickness, and misfortune. Participant CM42-2 stated that the most effective way to approach Nat worship is employing sacrificial animal offerings as a missiological lens to set them free from the bondage of suffering. Participant CM50 noted that promoting justice, peace, and love is the most effective way to share the gospel. Participant CF56 discovered that the most effective way to spread the gospel in the context of Nat worship is by sharing personal testimonies in which God answered Christians' prayers and mystical experiences. However, participants CM45 and CM46 viewed making friends with the Nat worshipers as the most important as there is a saying in Myanmar, "*Pokku khihma tayar myin*" meaning, friendship reveals the truth.

The difference between salvation in Christianity and Nat-Buddhism is crystal clear from the interview participant CM42-1. Salvation in Christianity is given, whereas liberation or salvation in Nat-Buddhism is earned. Moreover,

---

11. Schulz, *Mission from the Cross*, 138.
12. Bennett, *I Am Not Afraid*, 43.

Burmese Buddhists offer sacrifices out of fear, whereas Christian receive salvation through repentance and obedience to God. Therefore, it is crucial to preach the salvation of Jesus Christ that is received, not earned, just by accepting Jesus as Lord and Savior.

A careful perusal of the interview responses can be summed up in two categories: the interviewees presumed that the salvific message would be accepted if the Christian God had more power than Nat to deliver them from the bondage of sickness, misfortune, and poverty. Second, the Christian message of salvation will be accepted if Christians make friends with them and live with them peacefully. In other words, there are two possible approaches, the former is to confront the Nat or spirit worship, and the latter is to share the gospel by peaceful means. Therefore, there could be two possible outcomes if two approaches are employed. The first approach, confrontation, could result in winning souls for Christ, while the latter may end up in syncretism due to adherence and coexistence with other religions.

Question 10. What role does the church play in a context of Nat worship?

Participant CM42-1 suggested that the church plays a significant role in teaching its congregations about the possible contamination of Christianity with Nat worship. The church plays a vital role in encouraging believers not to be involved in animistic festival activities and not to embrace them as part of Christian activities. Participant CM42-2 stated that the church's role in the context of Nat worship is praise and worship that reflects the dances Nat worshipers perform in their festivals. Participant CF56 thought that the church must trust in the prevenient works of the Holy Spirit and follow his direction. The church should be a model for the Nat worshipers by performing spiritual exorcism and living the gospel and doing social charity work so that the church should be the light of the world. Participants CM45 and CM46 noted that because the greatest hindrance to the growth of churches in Myanmar is the spirit of Burmese-Buddhist nationalism, the churches should exercise spiritual power to break the chain.

Relating the role of the church to the mission of God must be defined missiologically because some Christians' approaches are too broad and others too narrow. For example, J. C. Hoekendijk marginalized the church's role in the mission of God as he prioritized the world's need. Hoekendijk's view led to the point that the church's activities must be under the guidance of the world rather than the triune God.¹³ Conversely, one of the researcher's former lecturers stated that Burmese Buddhists would not change their minds and therefore it was unnecessary to do evangelism among the Burmese Buddhists.

The importance of the *missio Dei* comes into play in the gap between the two views of the church in the world in relation to the mission of God. The goal of the mission of God is preaching the good news to the heathen through the church. The mission of the church is for the world and therefore, there must be a concrete connection between God, the church, and the world. Liberal Christians in Myanmar, as in other parts of the world, identify Christian churches with other religious institutions like Buddhist monasteries, mosques, or Hindu temples in the sense of recognizing shared spiritual or moral values as a common ground for social or community engagement. Therefore, it is imperative to note that the role of the Christian church in a Burmese Nat context is complex and multifaceted. Moreover, different Christian denominations have different approaches and practices, and the relationship between Christianity and Nat worship can be diverse and nuanced. Therefore, authentic Christians must maintain the Christian church as the locus of witnessing to Jesus as the Savior of the world.

The following section directly answers the research problem associated with the research questions. The research problem is that contemporary Myanmar Christian theologians understand that the mission of God needs to employ Nat worship principles in the context of Myanmar. The researcher combined the research and interview questions to respond to the research problem.

Research question 1: How ubiquitous is the Burmese primal religion (Nat worship) in Myanmar? Its subsequent operational questions and the structured interview questions delineated how prevalent Nat worship is and its impact. In response to the prevalence of Nat worship in the socioeconomic and religiopolitical life of the people, Simon Pau Khan En squarely bases his approach on his article *Building an Eco-Just Society*. He states that "The statues and images exhibited in the West at city squares and public centers have exposed the picture of human beings while in the east the arts have

---

13. Ott, *Mission of Church*, xv.

revealed the beauty of nature, landscape, forest, trees, rivers, etc. This is what determined theology in general and the doctrine of salvation in particular."[14]

En claims that the concept of Christian salvation formulated in the West mainly focused on human salvation, while in the East, religions appreciate nature, the manifestations, and the revelation of the deity through nature.[15] En is of the opinion that the Western-oriented doctrine of salvation lacks the nature aspect in the eastern-oriented doctrine of salvation. In other words, for En, salvation is through eco-justification or ecological soteriology. S. Mark Heim argues that salvation is a relationship of communion through Christ with God and with other creatures. According to his view, salvation is not just about being forgiven for sins, but also about being restored to a right relationship with God.[16]

The pervasiveness of Nat worship in Myanmar can be seen in the Burmese worldview. For example, the Myanmar governmental officials and religious leaders claimed that "We Burmese are Buddhists."[17] At the same time, the Burmese Buddhists still worship Nat, which is evident in the founding of a new city by King Mindon who was advised by the chief astrologer to slay a pregnant woman so that she might become the guardian spirit of his palace.[18] The amalgamation of two worldview systems in Myanmar endorses the missiological perspective of the existence of God. Although Burmese Buddhists have denied the doctrine of God, as William L. Craig asserts, "It is impossible to prove the existence of God, but we must prove by faith that God exists."[19] Since they believe in the existence of a supernatural being, that paves the way to introduce a Christian God.

Despite all against the belief in a personal God, the missionary Adoniram Judson deliberately translated the name of Christian God and the Holy Bible into Burmese successfully. Judson prefixed a phrase, "*thawarah,*" eternal and suffixed Thakhin, Lord, to *Phaya*, God, which means the eternal Lord God

---

14. En, "Eco-Just Society," 54.
15. En, "Eco-Just Society," 54.
16. Heim, *Depth of Riches*, 59.
17. Nyunt, *Mission amidst Pagodas*, 50.
18. Nisbet, *Burma Under British Rule*, 196.
19. Craig, *Reasonable Faith*, 93.

in his Burmese translation. The concept of Christian God, which Judson translated, is deeply intertwined with the concept of a Trinitarian God.[20]

According to Bailey Burmese Buddhists believe in Nat worship but reject Hindu's belief in reincarnation and soul. Simon Pau Khan En, a contemporary Christian theologian, asserts, "Nat worship enriches the Christian message and will serve as an effective source and a paradigm for fashioning ecumenical theology for Myanmar. Christians in Myanmar today have to learn the theology of human nature relationship from Nat worship."[21] However, Adoniram Judson called one who had a mixture of Burmese Nat worship and Buddhism a heathen.[22] A heathen referred to those who did not worship the God of Israel. Judson's reference to Burmese as a heathen is true when King Bagyidaw murdered his two hundred officials and two relatives in the form of idolatrous sacrifice to the Nat for his benefit.[23] Similarly, Perriere described Nat worship as based on myth and cult, which contributes to the institution of the pantheon of the Thirty-Seven held by Anawratha (1044–1077), the first Burmese king to rule over the entire Irrawaddy valley.[24]

The historical research and structured interview confirmed that Nat worship is omnipresent in Myanmar. However, several factors contribute to the different views of how Nat worship had impacted Christianity. So, all Buddhist interviewees who responded to the question viewed Nat worship as a traditional Burmese practice, but they held a variety of views on the degree to which Nat worship impacted Christianity. In contrast, others disagreed and said Buddhism and Nat worship are the same, which is inseparable in belief and practice. For example, participants BF34, BF26, and BM40 stated that there is no such thing as Nat worship in pure Buddhism even though it had an impact on Buddhism. However, a Buddhist participant BF37 believed that Nat, who guard Buddhist monks, is worthy of worship.

According to participant BF37, Nat who adhere to the Buddha's teaching are virtuous and they are worthy of worship. Burmese Nat-Buddhism is deeply ingrained in the sociocultural and religiopolitical lives of the

---

20. Bailey, *Adoniram Judson*, 61. See also, Moe, "Adoniram Judson," 270.
21. En, "Nat Worship," 1, 50.
22. Carver, "Significance of Adoniram Judson," 480.
23. Geiseman, *Men and Missions*, 9.
24. Perriere, "Burmese Nat," 45.

people and therefore it is tempting to shift to the belief that the way of the Christian life is the way of doing love and social justice. In response to this, the researcher sees the importance of Keener's observation that with Jesus's words: "I am the way, the truth, and the life," Jesus answers Thomas's question "The Father is where I am going, and I am how you will get there."[25] Jesus's words embody both the message and the authority of God's mission in the world. In contrast, En asserts that "Nat worship enriches the Christian messages and will serve as an effective source and a paradigm for fashioning ecumenical theology for Myanmar. Christians in Myanmar today have to learn the theology of human nature relationship from Nat worship."[26] From a theological perspective, one can draw some insights when examining, the relationship between human nature and Nat worship. However, there is a tendency that emphasizes the importance of the human desire, which could cause a bias toward the Christian missions.

Research question 2: How does Nat worship contrast with a Trinitarian theology of mission? Question 2 and its operational questions ask how a Trinitarian God contrasts with Nat worship. Adoniram Judson viewed Nat worship against the belief of Christianity as he stated, "we have found the country – Myanmar, as we expected in a most deplorable state, full of darkness, idolatry, and cruelty, full of commotion and uncertainty."[27]

However, Judson did not believe that Christianity should follow in the wake of Western civilization.[28] A Trinitarian framework was essential for Adoniram Judson, in implementing the mission of God in the context of Burmese Nat worship. Therefore, Judson thoroughly studied the name of God in order to translate it into the Burmese vernacular language. The Burmese name for God is *Phaya*, which refers to the Christian God, and the Buddhist monks and pagodas. However, further discussion on the Burmese sacred term *Phaya* and the Christian God may result in a very different understanding.

Newbigin profoundly responded to a pluralistic context by asking, who is Jesus? He is the Son, sent by the Father and anointed by the Spirit to be the bearer of God's kingdom to the nation. In contrast, a liberal Christian

---

25. Keener, *IVP Bible Background*, 291.
26. En, "Nat Worship," 50.
27. Edward, *Life of Adoniram Judson*, 79.
28. Edward, *Life of Adoniram Judson*, 82.

theologian in Myanmar contends, "Jesus showed us the way of God."[29] Jesus not only showed us the way, but He is the Way. In contrast to Zabik, Vicedom argued that Jesus Christ proves himself to be God and Lord of all men.[30]

John Flett rightly claims, "The problem of *missio Dei* is finally one of an undue breach between who God is in himself and who he is in his economy."[31] Flett summarizes this by noting that liberal theologians employ the doctrine of the Trinity as a means to critique the Christian mission associated with colonialism and Western cultural influence while, by doing so, they distance the Christian mission from a Trinitarian framework.[32] Myanmar is a pluralistic country, where minority religions, Christian, Hindu, and Muslim, coexisted with the majority religion, Buddhism, for centuries. Instead of protecting Jesus Christ's status as the Son of God and mediator between God and humanity, liberal theologians focus more on becoming a peaceful society by adhering to the ways of other faiths.

A Myanmar theologian, K. M. Y. Khawsiama, embraces the Buddhist views of *Phaya*, which denotes the Buddha, monks, and pagodas, and assimilates to the concept of Judson in naming the Christian God.[33] However, he does not consider Judson's use of the terms *Thawarah* – eternal, *Thakhin* – Lord, and *Phaya* – God. For example, Judson translated Zephaniah 3:17, "Yahweh your God is in your midst; a mighty warrior who saves. Your Lord God, the eternal God, is in your midst, the mighty God will save you"[34] as "သင်၏ဘုရားသခင် ထာဝရဘုရားသည်သင့်အလယ်၌ရှိ၍၊ တန်ခိုးကြီးသောဘုရသည်သင့်ကို ကယ်တင် တော်မူလိမ့်မည်။" (The Burmese Bible, 1835). Sadly, Myanmar Christian theologians do not pay enough attention to translating the name of God in the Myanmar context. Therefore, it widens the gap between God and the world, negatively impacting the sending of the Son and Spirit.[35] Three persons in the Godhead with particular entities and distinctive personality are inseparable. One cannot minimize the functionality of a triune God for mutual understanding and peaceful coexistence in a religiously pluralistic society.

---

29. Za Bik, "Universal Salvation," 24.
30. Vicedom, *Mission of God*, 33.
31. Flett, *Witness of God* 17.
32. Stetzer and Im, *Planting Missional Churches* 16.
33. Khawsiama, "Phayalogy," 17.
34. John, "Analysis of Adoniram Judson's," 70.
35. Flett, *Witness of God*, 18.

An anthropologist, Spiro, viewed that Nat worship amalgamated with Burmese Buddhism, and "Burmese Supernaturalism" as a combination of Nat worship and Buddhism.[36] Although Judson thought Burmese Nat worship contradicted Christianity, the belief in the existence of a supreme being could still be a platform for sharing the Christian faith. Participant CM42-1 viewed that without the concept of a supernatural being, it is impossible to approach the Burmese Buddhists. Participant CM42-1 believed the Holy Spirit plays a significant role in proclaiming the gospel to Nat worshipers. He added that Christian mission is a power encounter ministry (God and demons). U Hla Bu has suggested that Buddhism rejects all superstition, and the belief in a supernatural being is regarded as superstition. Buddha never claimed to save others but exhorted others to work out their own salvation.[37]

Participant CM50 stated that the doctrine of the Trinity plays a vital role in advancing the gospel to Nat worshipers because Nat worship had good spirits for which the Holy Spirit, the third person of the Trinity, can substitute. For Judson, the similarity in Nat worship and Christianity is still insufficient for one to make it into heaven. One must confess with his/her mouth that Jesus died for him/her.

Simon Pau Khan En holds the view that solidarity and the triune nature of the Godhead – Father, Son, and the Holy Spirit – could be an appropriate approach to Myanmar's religious diversity. This is because the Godhead, Father, Son, the Holy Spirit maintain their particular entity and distinctive personality, are one in essence and yet diverse in their personalities and have diverse functions in the economy of the Godhead.[38] What En means by this statement is that the nature and function of the triune God have adequately portrayed solidarity and diversities. The former is portrayed as one essence and the latter as their functionalities. The purpose of En in this approach is unity and solidarity in the midst of religious diversity in Myanmar, as mutuality is the basis for solidarity in the Godhead. The intention is not to advance the gospel of Christ but to have mutual understanding and peaceful coexistence amidst religious diversity.

---

36. Spiro, *Burmese Supernaturalism*, 148.
37. Bu, "Christian Encounter," 174.
38. En, "Solidarity amidst Diversity," 28.

Edmund Zabik, a Myanmar liberal Christian theologian, contends that Jesus showed us the way of God, which is the way to life and truth. Nevertheless, it is not so much by "getting associated with the "name-tag" of such words as 'Jesus Christ, Christian' as religious affiliation that saves but the whole-hearted reliving and embodying of the way of God that Christ has revealed to us (love, compassion, truthfulness, righteousness, purity of mind and motive,) as the key to Truth and Life."[39] Bik significantly minimizes a Trinitarian *missio Dei* by neglecting the name of Jesus Christ as a name tag for religious affiliation. In other words, Myanmar theologians Simon Pau Khan En and Edmund Za Bik largely dismissed a Trinitarian *missio* Dei framework in Christian missions because it did not fit into the Nat-Buddhist context.

Conversely, Newbigin, a Trinitarian theologian, responds, who is Jesus? He is the Son, sent by the Father and anointed by the Spirit to be the bearer of God's kingdom to the nations. For a Hindu, he is one of the *jeevanmuktas*, who have attained the full realization of the divine, and he is swamy or avatar. For Muslims, he is one of Allah's messengers.[40] In other words, neglecting the significant name of Jesus ruined a Trinitarian framework in Christian missions, and therefore it is incomplete.

This dissertation intends to advance the kingdom of God through the mission of God in the context of Myanmar. Therefore, the solidarity and unity of religious diversity and the universal salvation approach have failed to prove Christ as the Savior among people of other faiths. Vicedom asserts the universality of salvation that does not belong to a particular group of people but to all men. He adds, "if it were not the case, we could not speak of a reign of God, and the kingdom of God could not be the opposite of the kingdom of the world, which likewise demonstrates universality, unity, and closed ranks."[41] In contrast to Edmund Za Bik, Vicedom argued that Jesus Christ came to save and rescue all humankind.

Therefore, he proves himself to be God and Lord of all men. Vicedom's statement above, which is biblically sound, has yet to be recognized in the theology of missions. According to Za Bik, the concept of universal salvation failed to prove the attribution of God in Jesus Christ, the second person of

---

39. Za Bik, "Universal Salvation," 30.
40. Newbigin, *Open Secret*, 24.
41. Vicedom, *Mission of God*, 33–34.

the Trinity and the Savior of the world.[42] But Christian "mission is rooted in the mystery of the triune God, whose entire being is a communication and a giving of Himself to the world."[43] Since Jesus Christ is fully God, minimizing him from the triune God has seriously ruined the concept of a Trinitarian *missio Dei*. When the Trinitarian *missio Dei* is no longer in the Christian mission, it is no longer the mission of God.

Research question 3: What role does the church play in the context of Burmese Nat worship? Again, research question 3 encompasses the three operational questions of how the Christian church responds to Nat worshipers and the syncretistic Christians, and addresses the need for the everyday life of Christians in the context of Nat worship. It is fascinating to examine the methods Judson employed in his efforts to bring the gospel of Christ to the Burmese Nat worshipers. Simply "the sole weapons of his warfare were the old-fashioned truth, the existence of a personal and beneficent God, the fatal sinfulness of man, and salvation by faith in the Son of God, who came to seek and save that which was lost."[44] In addition to naming God to approach the Burmese Nat worshipers, Judson utilized *zayat* [tent] to contextualize the Christian church in the Burmese Buddhist context. Judson did not contextualize everything without analyzing whether it could harm the people or misrepresent the word of God. A Burmese Buddhist convert who later became an evangelist had adopted Judson's model. At first, he discovered that Christianity was heavily influenced by Western culture and that this could hinder Burmese people from becoming Christians. However, he learned the importance of contextualizing the gospel and utilized *zayat* in his ministry to the Burmese Buddhists. As a result, he became Myanmar's most successful Burmese evangelist and church planter.[45]

Judson employed four specific aspects in establishing the Christian church in Myanmar. First, Judson invented the *zayat* as a locus of witness for the gospel of Christ. Second, his approach was person-to-person evangelism in a roundtable model. Instead of learning how to use the elements of Nat worship, he invented *zayat* and utilized it for the church. Third, his strategies were

---

42. Za Bik, "Universal Salvation."

43. Schulz, *Mission from the Cross*, 37.

44. Judson, *Life of Adoniram Judson*, 82.

45. Fish, "Reclaiming Zayat Ministry," 3–4.

aligned with the New Testament model, which is grounded in the Scripture, so that it encounters with the world. Fourth, Judson was well equipped to teach the word of God so that he provided the word of God in the church. Fourth, the church Judson started was rooted in the history of the Christian church.

Conversely, Myanmar liberal theologians conceived that the Christian church symbolizes imperialism from the Western culture, which became parochialism and jeopardized losing its universal dimension. For example, Simon Pau Khan En appreciated what M. M. Thomas stated because Christ is the core content of the gospel, and the concept of Thomas's "Christ-Centered Syncretism" perfectly fits Myanmar.[46] In order to construct an authentic indigenous church, En and his contemporaries suggested changing the church building design from the Gothic architectural style to Buddhist temple designs. Moreover, En suggested that the structure of church membership should be different from that of the Western churches. According to En, churches have failed to emphasize the spiritual welfare of the members, as church pastors are more concerned with the numerical strength of the churches.

Participant CM42-1 suggested that the church must teach believers about Nat worship and their functions in light of the Bible. The church must encourage believers not to be involved in all the animistic ritual activities and thoughts. Participants CF56 and CM42-2 stated that the church should be a model for the Nat worshipers by performing spiritual practices of prayer and worship so that the church can be the light of the world. The Christian church should address the impact of Nat worship on Christians who still believe in palmistry, naming a child according to witch-masters, and future events such as marriage.

In contrast, En suggests that the Burmese Buddhists have a religious response while the other ethnic groups have a cultural response to the gospel. Hence a common basic approach to the Burmese people is the primal religion. However, En does not offer appropriate methods for the gospel to advance in the context of Nat worship. The author believes that the concept of primal religion helps the Burmese Nat worshipers understand the biblical worldview about their relationship with God and the concept of a supreme being. The Burmese worldview on a supreme being helps Burmese Nat worshipers

---

46. En, *Nat Worship*, 172.

understand the relationship with the natural world as they propitiate every object and landscape related to Nat. In contrast, the Christian God is the creator of those objects and landscapes whom the Burmese people worship.

In research question 3, the Christian church in the midst of the Burmese Nat worship plays a very important role in fulfilling the mission of God. The first American Protestant foreign missionary, Adoniram Judson, brought the gospel to the heathen land of Myanmar. He preached the gospel to the Burmese for five years without converting anyone to the Christian faith. Finally, he discovered how the church could play a vital role and invented the *zayat* [tent] concept and began to utilize it to further the gospel to the Burmese Buddhists. Judson converted hundreds of Burmese Buddhists from the sixth year onward to the Christian faith.

Research question 3 is related to the central role of the ecclesiological dimension of Christian activities inside and outside the church. Dr. Schulz helpfully stated that, "the mission of the Church flows from the theocentric and trinitarian impulse and revelation itself. The mission of God in time continues through the activity of human preachers and workers throughout the world, while the success of mission remains God's alone."[47] Myanmar liberal theologians frankly oppose the central role of the church in the mission of God by imitating Nat worship over a Trinitarian framework. However, the mission of God is fulfilled through the church's activity as it preaches the Word to the unbelievers. As Dr. Schulz persuasively stated, the church should imitate the triune God rather than the local deities. If the Christian church withdraws from the Trinitarian framework and imitates the national deities, it is impossible to talk about the mission of the church because it should only flow from the Trinitarian *missio Dei*.

Detaching the mission's activities from the church would seriously corrupt the whole concept of the church. "The truth is that the church is not the church in any New Testament sense unless it is a mission . . . Emil Brunner famously phrases, 'the church exists by mission as fire exists by burning.'"[48] The church is still in the world; how to be in the world as the church is very fundamental, especially in the pluralistic country of Myanmar. Therefore, as Johannes Blauw sums it up, "The people of God in both Old and New

---

47. Schulz, *Mission from the Cross*, 96.
48. Ott, ed., *Mission of Church*, xviii.

Testaments are a missionary people called and set apart by God as his agents of righteousness and redemption in the world and among all nations."[49] Being the church in the world is challenging because it needs to integrate with the world in biblically acceptable ways.

The Lausanne Movement defines evangelism as a commission to "the whole church to take the whole gospel to the whole world, as was put forward at the WCC Assembly in New Delhi in 1961."[50] One of the Lausanne movement's significant shifts was to include social justice as an integral part of the holistic mission of the church. As a result, it became challenging for the church to prioritize physical or spiritual needs. The point of departure for liberal Christians from the evangelical Christianity is to prioritize the physical needs so that the physical needs of social justice and peaceful coexistence could advance the gospel of Christ. The researcher argues that prioritizing the church's mission should refer to the Bible. As a result, according to Jesus Christ, the primary concern is meeting spiritual needs over physical and material things; as Matthew 6:33 puts it, "But seek ye first the Kingdom of God and his righteousness; and all these things [physical needs] shall be added unto you" (KJV).

In his monumental work, Christopher Wright, a former chair of the Lausanne Movement, sums up the church's mission as one that addresses creation care, reconciliation, social justice, and cultural engagement. Wright prioritizes reconciliation over social justice and cultural engagement. The researcher agrees with Wright that reconciliation between man and God is the primary mission of the church, and then follow social justice and peaceful coexistence. Therefore, the goal of the mission of the church is to convert the people into the likeness of Christ. That is the ultimate missionary purpose of the church.

---

49. Ott, *Mission of Church*, xviii.
50. Ott, *Mission of Church*, xxiv.

CHAPTER 5

Research Summary, Conclusions, Implications, and Recommendations

This dissertation examines the efforts of contemporary Myanmar theologians to reconcile Nat worship with Christianity. The primary aim is to develop a theology of mission by grounding the gospel in Myanmar's cultural context and addressing idolatry influenced by Nat worship. The study uses qualitative methods, including historical research and structured interviews, to gather data about Buddhism and Christianity in Myanmar.

First of all, by using the categories in the phenomenology of religion as described by Plantinga, the researcher discovered the inner structure and elements of Nat worship and Buddhism – that they are not mere primal religions but deeply interwoven in the religious system. And also, by utilizing a qualitative coding described by Moustake, the researcher found specific elements of Nat worship, including ritual water and sacred objects, the Burmese Nat-Buddhists apply in their daily life. The research methodologies employed in this study help the researcher with specific concepts, ideas, and reasons that support the argument. After understanding the elements and essence of Nat worship in Burmese Buddhists and liberal Christians, the researcher identified and understood the phenomenon of Burmese Nat worship elements that are incompatible with the Christian faith.

Further, through historical research and interviews, the researcher recognized that liberal Christians in Myanmar recommend a syncretistic approach to the Burmese Nat-Buddhists to avoid conflict and tension. The research findings confirmed that the elements of Burmese Nat worship do not enrich the Christian missions but harm the growth and flourishing of Christian churches. Also, the research finding demonstrated that interreligious dialogue is the alternative way for liberal Christians to avoid conflict, which is based out of fear. The research and interview questions addressed the research problem, and common themes regarding the impact of Burmese traditional religion on their sociocultural and religiopolitical life.

In the same way, evangelical Christians asserted that Christian missions must aim at conversion, while liberal Christians encouraged interfaith dialogue as a necessity for religious and ethnic reconciliation. In the same vein, there has been increasing evidence that conversion to Christianity is unnecessary from the liberal point of view, while conversion is the central theme of the mission of God for evangelical Christianity. Liberal Christians prioritize religious and cultural values, while evangelical Christians prioritize individual conversion to Christianity even at the cost of suffering. After examining the historical research and structured interviews, the researcher concluded that the mission of God through a Trinitarian *missio Dei* and Christocentric and ecclesio-centric viewpoint is the only legitimate ground, and the liberal approach to utilize elements of Nat worship for Christian missions is insufficient.

Conclusions

This dissertation has proposed a theology of mission as the framework for responding to contemporary theologians' attempt to reconcile Nat worship with Christianity in Myanmar. The author argued that the message of the gospel is the message of reconciliation "that God was reconciling the world to himself in Christ, not counting people's sin against them. And he has committed to us the message of reconciliation" (2 Cor 5:19). This thesis statement should be a wake-up call to the Christian mission in Myanmar. Contemporary theologians' attempt to reconcile Nat worship with Christianity in Myanmar raises thought-provoking questions. Therefore, a clear demarcation between the Christian faith and Burmese Buddhist-Nat worship is already established.

Reconciling Christian faith with anything that goes against biblical teachings is pervasive and challenging. It is essential to remain vigilant and rooted in the principles and guidelines outlined in the Bible to avoid diluting or compromising the core tenets of the Christian faith. This includes being cautious about syncretism and ensuring that the integrity of the biblical message is upheld in all aspects of reconciliation and engagement with other beliefs.

The term "the mission of God, *missio Dei*" implies that "God has a mission, a sending to the world, but God is also in himself sending, the triune God, who as Son and Holy Spirit is sent into the world."[1] The author argued that the contemporary liberal Christians' attempt to reconcile Burmese Nat worship with Christianity is no longer adequate. Because, grounding mission in the doctrine of the Trinity distances contemporary theologians' attempt to reconcile Nat worship with the Christian faith.

From a biblical point of view, reconciling Nat worship with Christianity endangers the Christian faith because there is only one message of reconciliation between God and man. That is, the alienated sinners can be reconciled to God through Jesus Christ. Reconciliation with God is possible through the sacrificial atonement of Jesus Christ. In other words, reconciliation of Nat worship with Christian faith goes against a biblical perspective of reconciliation. There is no other way to heaven except Jesus Christ. That is the ultimate purpose of the Great Commission. That is what Christians teach, preach, live, and some even die for. Reconciliation is the will of God, reconciliation is by the act of forgiveness, reconciliation is by the obedience of faith (2 Cor 5:20).

The researcher would like to recapitulate what has been discussed in this dissertation. First, fulfilling the Great Commission of Jesus Christ, the mission of God, is the most important task for Christians worldwide. It is difficult to determine how to fulfill the mission of God in the context of Burmese Nat worship. However, the researcher argued that the fulfillment of the mission of God is through preaching the gospel rooted in the triune God. Therefore, a Trinitarian mission of God refers to God's redemptive work accomplished by the three persons of the Trinity.

Second, the researcher responded to liberal Christians' failure to explain human suffering because they largely minimized the suffering of Christ as a *sine qua non* for the redemption of this world. Since the Burmese Nat-Buddhists view the tragic, frightening, and brutal death of Jesus as only due to his own sin, liberal Christians shifted their approach to interfaith dialogue to attain temporary peaceful coexistence. The researcher claimed that authentic Christians "know the transcendent nature of the Trinity through

---

1. Flett, *Witness of God*, 36.

the incarnation of Christ by the Spirit."[2] The power of the gospel lies in the suffering of Christ, but the Burmese Buddhist cannot see it as a ransom for many. Liberal Christians in Myanmar misinterpreted and misunderstood the meaning of Christ's suffering by neglecting it as a means for conversion to Christianity.

Third, the researcher claimed that the *zayat* of Adoniram Judson plays a vital role for Christian church amid Buddhist-Nat worship in Myanmar. Judson did not shy away from the mission of God despite the number of challenges he faced in a heathen land. Scholars such as Leslie Newbigin support this claim: "We have corrupted the word Church by constantly using it in a non-missionary sense."[3] This is true when liberal Christians in Myanmar do not distinguish the church from the cultural values of the people. There is the evil side of the culture, which Christians need to abandon when they convert to Christianity. Liberal Christians view this as an attempt to destroy the local culture. Therefore, the researcher concluded that the mission of God established the most important institution – the church.

Fourth, the researcher proposed the Scriptures and a Trinitarian *missio Dei* as a proper starting point for a theology of mission. The researcher adequately demonstrated the role of the Trinitarian concept, and the mission of God rooted in Scripture that excluded any possible way for syncretism in Christianity, such as the concept that all religions lead to the same destination. Employing a Trinitarian framework as a response to liberal Christian missions in Myanmar distances Christian missions from syncretistic Christianity. Therefore, the missionary Adoniram Judson constantly preached the triune God to distinguish him from other gods. The ultimate purpose in employing a Trinitarian framework in the mission of God is for the conversion of Burmese Nat-Buddhists in Myanmar.

Implications

The structured interviews and historical research have shown important themes. One is that the liberal Christians in Myanmar have attempted to reconcile Christianity with Burmese Nat worship. Also, the researcher has

---

2. Moe, "Trinitarian Theology," 3, 253.
3. Newbigin, *One Body*, 42.

shown what a theology of mission is based on Scripture, and what a theology of mission is not. What does the researcher mean by what a theology of mission is not? The unfortunate thing is that some liberal Christians in Myanmar dismiss the Bible as the word of God and do not think it has meaningful implications for everyday life. A Christian mission which is not based on Scripture and a triune God is not a theology of mission.

The contemporary liberal Christians in Myanmar believed something else was necessary for salvation in addition to what Christ had done on the cross. For example, liberal Christians in Myanmar embrace the elements of Burmese Nat worship to enrich the redemptive work of Christ, and that his mission will be more effective for Nat worshipers. The researcher's suggestion is that Myanmar churches should practice spirit exorcism to drive the spirit [Nat] out of the people and community. The interview participant CM42-1 and research findings confirmed that the Burmese people worship Nat out of fear, and the power encounter with the Holy Spirit would be the most effective way to share the redemptive work of Christ.

For liberal Christians, Jesus is an example of faith as a "mild-mannered exponent of a non-discriminating love."[4] However, Jesus is not merely an example of faith and life. He is our Savior, the object of our faith. In this sense, the liberal views of Christ vastly diminish the essence of the economy of the Trinity. The researcher's argument is deeply rooted in three themes: the need for a Trinitarian theology of mission, the mission of Christ, and the church's mission. The researcher suggests that a proper understanding of the gospel must be rooted in a Trinitarian theology of mission, which emphasizes the role of the Father, Son, and Holy Spirit in salvation. The mission of Christ displays the centrality of Jesus Christ in salvation. The researcher recommends that a proper understanding of the gospel must be based on the belief that Jesus is the Savior of the world and that salvation is only possible through him. This view contrasts with liberal Christianity, which often sees Jesus as just one of many spiritual leaders and denies the exclusivity of salvation through him.

The researcher encourages that churches in Myanmar should be seen as a place of worship, and as a community of believers who work together to carry out God's mission in the world. The mission of the church plays a significant role in spreading the gospel. In summary, evangelical Christians deliberately

---

4. Machen, *Christianity and Liberalism*, 37.

distinguish between converted and nominal Christians, where the former has abandoned the traditional religious practices of Myanmar, and the latter still holds on to their previous practices. Unfortunately, Myanmar's liberal Christian leaders prioritize peace with other religions, which can lead to a temporary peace in society, but not eternal peace with God.

As one can see, the Myanmar liberal Christians syncretized Christianity with the Burmese Nat-Buddhist systems. The researcher succinctly examined the belief systems of Nat worship, Theravada Buddhism, and Christianity and their relationship with each other through historical research and structured interview. Therefore, the researcher suggests that the Christian mission must start with Scripture and the Trinity, which are inseparably linked because human error can separate the Christian mission from the Scripture and a Trinitarian framework. David Bosch contends that mission is grounded on a Trinitarian framework in the claim that the Father sent the Son, and the Father and the Son sent the Holy Spirit.[5]

The Burmese worldview is constructed on a system of supernatural beings intermingled within their belief systems, Nat worship, but they rejected the Christian God as a source of knowledge. American anthropologist Spiro Melford explained that the Burmese Nat worship is based on supernaturalism. The researcher has shown that the supernatural concept is a point of context for a theology of mission which is inextricably linked to a Trinitarian theology of mission, the mission of the church, and the mission of Christ. The researcher suggests the view of the contemporary liberal Christians in Myanmar is insufficient and non-biblical.

Based on the structured interviews and research findings, there are two views on the missiological approach in the context of Burmese Nat worship. Liberal Christians view cultural context as the starting point for a theology of mission, and evangelical Christians view the Scripture as the starting point – these are two key differences concerning a theology of mission between liberal and evangelical Christianity in Myanmar. The researcher proposes the need for a truly biblical worldview based on a Trinitarian theology of mission to respond to liberal Christians in line with Wright's claims that the entire Bible is about the mission of God.[6]

---

5. Bosch, *Transforming Mission*, 400.
6. Wright, *Mission of God*, 29.

Because Nat-Buddhism has been part and parcel of the national life of the Burmese people for two thousand years, it indeed continues to shape all dimensions of life. Amid the political struggle and ethnic crisis in Myanmar, Buddhist nationalism continues to shape the liberal Christian view of the church. This is contrary to Judson's suggestions: "The churches of Jesus will soon supplant these idolatrous monuments, and the chanting of the devotees of Buddha will die away before the Christian hymn of praise."[7]

Worldview is a person's overall perspective on life, including beliefs, values, and assumptions about the world. Sharing the Christian worldview in a respectful and non-judgmental way can create opportunities to explore different worldviews and share the Christian message in a meaningful way. For example, when the Christian faith successfully transforms the worldview of primitive practices, though they hold different beliefs or values, they can connect with the Christian faith on a deeper level that shapes their belief system. An evangelical worldview will allow the Bible to shape how we approach everything else in our beliefs (what a human being is, how we should think about history and science etc) while a non-biblical worldview will see the Bible through human experience, and allow our human experience to shape what we believe about the Bible.[8]

Recommendations for Further Research

A further question arising from this research is what missiological methodologies should be employed to achieve a theology of mission in a better way. The researcher recommends that Christian missionaries, pastors, and evangelists in Myanmar should utilize a Trinitarian *missio Dei* deeply rooted in Scripture for the conversion of the people. The researcher's suggestion did not happen in a vacuum but after evaluating the past and present missiological methodologies. Liberal Christians in Myanmar recommend a syncretistic approach as the legitimate strategy that largely sidelines the word of God as the core and source of the mission of God.

The researcher suggests that Christian pastors, evangelists, and missionaries have a proper study of the concept of God in the context of Nat worship.

---

7. Armstrong, "Judson's Successors," 61.
8. Mock, *Old Testament Survey*, 24.

While it may be true that Western missionaries did not fully understand the concept of the supreme being, it is not appropriate to dismiss it as "heathenism" without attempting to understand its cultural significance and context. Only if Christians approach with curiosity and respect, seeking to understand their cultural significance and context, will they accept the supreme being that can pave the way to accept the classical Christian doctrine of the Trinity. The vision of the researcher for Christianity in Myanmar's future is that conversion to Christianity will no longer involve syncretism with Buddhist-Nat worship systems.

Therefore, the researcher recommends re-establishing the lost Christian mission of God through a rigorous examination of Scripture and a Trinitarian framework. It is extremely important to rediscover the value of Scripture and a Trinitarian *missio Dei* which has lost its meaning in a pluralistic society. A Scripture based Christian theology of mission will help shift away from the paradigm that liberal Christians had proposed for doing Christian mission in Myanmar.

Also, the researcher recommends that since Nat worship is spirit-based, the concept of spirit plays a vital role in manifesting the Spirit of God. The Burmese Nat worship is a traditional form of an animistic belief system that involves the worship of various spirits which are believed to have the power to influence various aspects of human life, including health, prosperity, and fortune. Rather than simply dismissing these practices as "heathenism," it is important to transform them into Christian practices of spiritual exorcism. For example, Dr. Robert Bennett successfully utilizes the Malagasy Lutheran concept of the biblical reality of demons and exorcism.[9]

Like many other Christian denominations, the Lutheran church has a tradition of dealing with spiritual issues, including those related to demon possession. Dr. Bennett asserts, "Daily the exorcists of the Malagasy Lutheran Church continue to drive out demons that have possessed the people."[10] This reveals that people are joining the Lutheran church because the Lutheran Church is able to deal with the spiritual concerns of the people. In the same vein, if Myanmar churches can deal with and drive out demons that have

---

9. Bennett, *I Am Not Afraid*, 99.
10. Bennett, *I Am Not Afraid*, 106.

possessed the people, more Myanmar people might join Christian churches, rather than liberal Christian embracing Nat worship.

This study is a single attempt to respond to liberal Christians' attempt to reconcile Nat worship with Christianity in the context of Myanmar. It deals with the encounter between Christian mission and Burmese Nat worship. Therefore, there are a number of other subject areas worthy of further research. For example, spiritual exorcism would be both an interesting and valuable theological research for Christian churches. It is also worthwhile to do further research on Trinitarian theology in a pluralistic society concerned with pneumatology and Christology.

The researcher's suggestion for further research recognizes that interreligious dialogue for peaceful coexistence is a complex and multifaceted issue that requires a nuanced understanding of the local context. While liberal Christians may have a particular approach to interfaith dialogue, it is possible that their methods may not be effective in certain cultural and religious settings. It is the researcher's assertion that the Christian can promote reconciliation and peaceful coexistence through the guidance of the triune God rather than adopting and accepting the principles of other faiths.

Throughout this research work, many issues have been mentioned without detailed analysis. While they are important to Christian mission in a Burmese Nat worship context, these issues need further research. A number of suggestions and questions for further research have emerged, including but not limited to the following. More research is needed with respect to the sociocultural and religious identity of Myanmar people in the context of Buddhism, Christianity, Hinduism, and Islam. Related to the above is the need for research on the Burmese worldview. It will give perspectives on how Burmese Buddhists and Nat worshipers would help in developing a better way for fulfilling the Great Commission in Myanmar.

Therefore, the researcher has suggested in this dissertation that Myanmar Christian churches should use a Trinitarian *missio Dei* pattern to strengthen Myanmar Christianity and solve the problem of syncretism. This then will be an adequate response to the challenge of contemporary liberal Christians in Myanmar. The elements of Nat worship described in this dissertation need to be paid careful attention as it is critical to eliminate the back-door loss of Christianity. The researcher recommends that using the methodology in this dissertation is useful for Christians to find out the elements of Nat worship that have weakened the Christian missions. Therefore, the discovered concepts in the research may fit the needs of liberal Christian leaders who profess to love Jesus but disdain the Trinitarian framework for Christian missions.

Bibliography

Al-Yahsubi, Qadi Iyad Ibn Musa. *Muhammad Messenger of Allah*. Translated by Aisha Abarrahman Bewley. Norwich: Diwan Press, 2011.

Alexandra, Kaloyanides. "Show Us Your God": Marilla Baker Ingalls and the Power of Religious Objects in Nineteenth-Century Burma. *Religion* 7, no. 81 (2016): 1.

Allen, Roland. *Missionary Methods: St. Paul's or Ours*. Grand Rapids: Eerdmans Publishing, 1962.

Allerton, Catherine. "Introduction: Spiritual Landscapes of Southeast Asia." *Anthropological Forum* 3, no. 19 (2009): 234–51.

Anderson, Courtney. *To the Golden Shore: The Life of Adoniram Judson*. Grand Rapids: Zondervan, 1956.

Armstrong, Ruth M. "Judson's Successors in the Heyday of Burma Missions." *Missiology: An International Review* 23, no. 1 (January 1995): 61.

Aung, Maung Htin. *A History of Burma*. New York: Columbia University Press, 1967.

Bailey, Faith Coxe. *Adoniram Judson, Missionary to Burma 1813–1850*. Chicago: Moody Press, 1955.

Bauer, David R., and Robert A. Traina. *Inductive Bible Study: A Comparative Guide to the Practice of Hermeneutics*. Grand Rapids: Baker Academy, 2011.

Bawihrin, Thla-Awr. "The Impact of Missionary Christianity on the Chins." D.Min diss., Ashland Theological Seminary, 2002.

Bennett, Robert. *I Am Not Afraid: Demon Possession and Spiritual Warfare*. St. Louis: Concordia Publishing Press, 2013.

Bickman, Leonard, and Debra J. Rog. *Handbook of Applied Social Research Methods*. Thousand Oaks: SAGE, 1998.

Boff, Leonardo, and Clodovis Boff. *Introducing Liberation Theology*. Maryknoll: Orbis Books, 2011.

Bosch, David. *Transforming Mission: Paradigm Shifts in Theology of Mission*. Maryknoll: Orbis Books, 2014.

Boston University, School of Theology. "Voetius Gisbertus (1589–1676), a Dutch Reformed Theologian and the First Protestant to Write a Comprehensive Theology of Mission." Accessed May 2022. https://www.bu.edu/missiology/missionary-biography/t-u-v/voetius-gisbertus-gijsbert-voet-1589-1676/.

Bradshaw, Bruce. *Change Across Cultures: A Narrative Approach to Social Transformation*. Grand Rapids: Baker Academy, 2002.

Bu, U. Hla. "The Christian Encounter with Buddhism in Burma." *International Review of Missions* 47, no. 186 (1958): 174.

Bwa, Saw Hlaing. "Challenges of the Change in Myanmar and New Theological Reflections." A Paper Presented at the Judson Research Center in Yangon, January 2014.

Carver, W. O. "The Significance of Adoniram Judson." *The Review and Expositor* 10, no. 4, (October 1913): 480.

Cary, Philip. *Outward Signs: The Powerlessness of External Things in Augustine's Thought*. Oxford: Oxford University Press, 2008.

Cing, Luan Za. *Tedim Gam Christian Taangthu: Rev. Sukte T. Hau Go Taangthu*. Yangon: Hebron Printing Press, 2010.

Coomaraswamy, Ananda K. *Buddha and the Gospel of Buddhism*. New York: Harper Torchbooks, 1916.

Coupland, Reginald. *British Empire History*. London: Hutchinson & Pub., 1950.

Craig, William L. *Reasonable Faith: Christian Faith and Apologetics*. Wheaton: Crossway, 2008.

Creswell, John W., and J. David Creswell. *Research Design: Qualitative, Quantitative, and Mixed Methods Approaches*. Los Angeles: SAGE, 2018.

Coulibaly, Issiaka. "2 Corinthians." In *Africa Bible Commentary: A One-Volume Commentary Written by 70 African Scholars*, edited by Adeyemo, Tokunboh. Grand Rapids: Zondervan, 2010.

Curtis, Steve. "Worldviews in Myanmar: A Missiological Perspective." *Mission Studies* 35 (1) (2018): 57–83.

Dahlin, Emma. "Email Interviews: A Guide to Research Design and Implementation." *International Journal of Qualitative Methods* 20, no. 1–10 (2021): 1.

Dhammananda, Sri K. *What Buddhists Believe*. Taipei, the Corporate Body of the Buddha Educational Foundation, 1993.

Dingrin, La Seng. "The Conflicting Legacy of Adoniram Judson: Appropriating and Polemicizing against Burmese Buddhism." *Missiology: An International Review* 37, no. 4 (October 2009): 485–97.

Doe, Saw Maung. *Discipling the Church: A Study of Christian Education in the Anglican Church of Myanmar*. Oxford: Regnum Books International, 2015.

Dorp, Arend Van. *Ethnic Diversity and Reconciliation: A Missional Model for the Church in Myanmar*. Carlisle: Langham Global Library, 2022.

Dyrness, William A., and Veli-Matti Karkkainen. *Global Dictionary of Theology.* Downers Grove: IVP, 2008.

Elliston, Edgar J. *Introduction to Missiological Research Design.* Pasadena: William Carey Library, 2011.

Elwell, Walter A., and Robert W. Yarbrough. *Encountering the New Testament.* Grand Rapids: Baker Books, 1984.

Elwood, Douglas J., ed. *What Asian Christians Are Thinking.* Quezon City: New Day Publishers, 1976.

Emma, "Qualitative Coding Tutorial: How to Code Qualitative Data for Analysis" *Youtube,* January 27, 2022, 04:16 to 05:33, https://www.youtube.com/watch?v=8MHkVtE_sVw, accessed on 4 April 2023, 10 p.m. EST.

En, Simon Pau Khan. "Nat Worship: A Paradigm for Doing Ecumenical Theology in Myanmar." *Asia Journal of Theology* 8, no. 1 (1994): 47–49.

———. "The Quest for Authentic Myanmar Contextual Theology." *RAY: MIT Journal of Theology* 3, (2002): 84.

———. "Building an Eco-Just Society." *RAYS: MIT, Journal of Theology* 3, no. Issues, 14 (2004): 54.

———. *Nat Worship: A Paradigm for Doing Contextual Theology in Myanmar.* Yangon: MIT, Judson Research Center, 2012.

———. "Solidarity amidst Diversity." *RAYS: MIT Journal of Theology* 5 (2014): 28.

Fish, Lazarus. "Reclaiming the Zayat Ministry: Witness to the Gospel among Burmese Buddhists in Myanmar." Dissertation, Asbury Theological Seminary, July 2002.

Fleet, John. *The Witness of God: The Trinity, Missio Dei, Karl Barth, and the Nature of Christian Community.* Grand Rapids: Eerdmans, 2010.

Flemming, Dean. *Contextualization in the New Testament: Patterns for Theology and Mission.* Downers Grove: IVP, 2005.

Fullan, Michael. *Leading in a Culture of Change.* San Francisco: Jossey-Bass, 2001.

Gadamer, Hans-Georg. *Truth and Method.* London: Continuum, 2006.

Geiseman, Ott Albert. *Men and Missions: Consuming Love, An Account of the Life and Work of Adoniram Judson, Missionary to Burma.* St. Louis: Concordia Publishing House, 1929.

Gooding, David, and John Lennox. *Being Truly Human: The Limits of Our Worth, Power, Freedom and Destiny.* Belfast: Myrtlefield House, 2018.

———. *Claiming to Answer: How One Person Became the Response to Our Deepest Question.* Belfast: Myrtlefield House, 2019.

———. *Questioning Our Knowledge.* Belfast: Myrtlefield, 2019.

———. *Suffering Life's Pain: Facing the Problem of Moral and Natural Evil.* Belfast: Myrtlefield, 2019.

Gulati, Bush. "The Politics of Buddhism in Burma." *Youtube*. http://www.youtube.com/watch?v=gsP0Q6YW3Bs, 14:40 minutes, published on 24 November 2007.

Gundry, Robert H. *Commentary on the New Testament*. Peabody: Hendrickson, 2010.

Gutierrez, Gustavo. *A Theology of Liberation: History, Politics, and Salvation*. Maryknoll: Orbis Books, 2016.

Harmon, Steven R. "Adoniram Judson, Baptist, the Whole Church, and God's Mission" *International Bulletin of Mission Research*. 14, no. 2 (2014): 41.

Harvey, G. E. *History of Burma*. London: Longmans, Green and Company, 1925.

Heim, Mark S. *Salvations: Truth and Difference in Religion*. Maryknoll: Orbis Books, 1997.

———. *The Depth of the Riches: A Trinitarian Theology of Religious Ends*. Grand Rapids: Eerdmans, 2001.

———. *Saved from Sacrifice: A Theology of the Cross*. Grand Rapids: Eerdmans, 2006.

Henry, Matthew, and Thomas Scott. *Matthew Henry's Concise Commentary*. Oak Harbor: Logos Research System, 1997.

Hick, John. "Religious Pluralism and Salvation. Faith and Philosophy" *Journal of the Society of Christian Philosophers* 5 (1988): 293.

Hiebert, Paul G. *Anthropological Insights for Missionaries*. Grand Rapids: Baker Book House, 1985.

Hmung, Zo Tum. "After the 2021 Military Coup in Myanmar/Burma." *Report of the Chin Association of Maryland* (October 2021): 19–21.

Hodges, Charles. *Systematic Theology*. New York: Charles Scribner & Company, 1873.

Hubbard, Ethel Daniel. *Ann of Ava*. Freeport: Books for Libraries Press, 1941.

Isaac, Munther. *From Land to Lands, from Eden to the Renewed Earth: A Christ-Centered Biblical Theology of the Promised Land*. Carlisle: Langham Academic, 2015.

Jamieson, Robert, A. R. Fausset, and David Brown. *A Commentary, Critical and Explanatory on the Whole Bible*. Oak Harbor: Logos Research Systems, 1997.

John, Hans de Jong. "An Analysis of Adoniram Judson's Translation of Zephaniah." *SAGE Journals: United Bible Societies* 68, no. 1 (2017): 70.

Judson, Edward. *The Life of Adoniram Judson*. New York: Anson D. F. Randolph, 1883.

Kasali, David. "Romans." In *Africa Bible Commentary: A One-Volume Commentary Written by 70 African Scholars*, edited by Adeyemo, Tokunboh. Grand Rapids: Zondervan, 2010.

Keane, Webb. *Christian Moderns: Freedom & Fetish in the Mission Encounter*. Los Angeles: University of California Press, 2007.

Keen, S., M. Lomeli-Rodriguez, and H. Joffe. "From Challenge to Opportunity: Virtual Qualitative Research During COVID-19 and Beyond." SAGE *International Journal Qualitative Methods* 21 (2022): 1–11.

Keener, Craig. *The IVP Bible Background Commentary: New Testament*. Downers Grove: IVP, 2014.

Khai, Ciin Sian. *Rediscovering Religious Human Rights in Myanmar*. Saarbrueken: Lambert Academic Publishing, 2012.

Khawsiama, K. M. Y. "Jesus Christ: the Savior and Liberator in the Burmese Buddhist Cultural Context," *Contextual Engagement*, 188.

———. "Phayalogy: A Study of Adoniram Judson's Naming God as Phaya from a Christian-Buddhist View in Myanmar Context." *Asia Journal of Theology* 28, no. 1 (April 2014): 16–34.

King, Winston L. *Buddhism and Christianity: Some Bridges of Understanding*. London: Georg Allen and Unwin, 1963.

Kitamori, Kozah. *Theology of the Pain of God*. Richmond: John Knox Press, 1965.

Köstenberger, Andreas J., and Peter T. O'Brien. *Salvation to the Ends of the Earth: A Biblical Theology of Mission*. Downers Grove: IVP, 2001.

Kraft, Charles H. *Anthropology for Christian Witness*. Maryknoll: Orbis Books, 2003.

Luther, Martin. *A Commentary on St. Paul's Epistle to the Galatians*. Wittenberg: University of Wittenberg, 1535.

Machen, J. Gresham. *Christianity and Liberalism*. Grand Rapids: Eerdmans, 2009.

Mang, Pum Za. "Christianity and Ethnic Identity in Burma." *Journal of Church and State* 61, no. 1 (Winter 2019): 93.

Mathiesen, Gaylan Kent. *A Theology of Mission: Challenges and Opportunities in Northeast Asia*. Minneapolis: Lutheran University Press, 2006.

Mathieson, Alfred. *Judson of Burma: The Heroic Pioneer Missionary to the Burmese, Who for the Welfare of Others Faced Every Peril and Dared Every Danger*. London: Pickering & Inglis, 1924.

McHale, Sue. "A Practical Guide to the E-Mail Interview." *Qualitative Health Research* 17, no. 10 (2007): 14–15.

Michael, Kisskalt. "Mission as Convivence: Life Sharing and Mutual Learning in Mission Inspirations from German Missiology." European Baptist Theological Teachers' Conference, 16–19 July 2020.

Mock, Dennis J. *Old Testament Survey*. Atlanta: Bible Training Center, 1989.

Moe, David Thang. "Adoniram Judson: A Dialectical Missionary Who Brought the Gospel [not God] and Gave the Bible to the Burmese." *Missiology: An International Review* 45, no. 3 (April 2017): 270.

———. "A Trinitarian Theology of Religions: Themes and Issues in Evangelical Approaches." *Evangelical Review of Theology* 41, no. 3 (2017): 253.

Moustakes, Clark. *Phenomenological Research Methods*. London: SAGE, 1994.

Nash, June C. *Practicing Ethnography in a Globalizing World: Anthropological Odyssey,* 2nd ed. Lehman: Alta Mira, 2007.

Nehrbass, Kenneth. *Christianity and Animism in Melanesia: Four Approaches to Gospel and Culture.* Pasadena: William Carey Library, 2012.

Newbigin, Leslie. *One Body, One Gospel, One World: The Christian Mission Today.* London: IMC, 1958.

———. *The Gospel in a Pluralistic Society.* Grand Rapids: Eerdmans, 1989.

———. *The Open Secret: An Introduction to the Theology of Mission.* Grand Rapids: Eerdmans, 1995.

———. *Signs Amid the Rubble.* Grand Rapids: Eerdmans, 2003.

Niebuhr, H. Richard. *Christ and Culture.* New York: Harper Torchbooks, 1956.

Nisbet, John. *Burma Under British Rule and Before.* London: Westminster, 1901.

Nissen, Johannes. *New Testament and Mission: Historical and Hermeneutic Perspectives.* Frankfurt: Peter Lang, 2004.

Nyunt, Peter Thein. *Mission amidst Pagodas: Contextual Communication of the Gospel in the Burmese Buddhist Context.* Carlisle: Langham Academic, 2014.

Ott, Craig, ed. *The Mission of the Church: Five Views of Conversation.* Grand Rapids: Baker Academy, 2016.

Ott, Craig, and Harold Netland. *Globalizing Theology: Belief and Practice in an Era of the World Christianity.* Grand Rapids: Baker Academy, 2006.

Ott, Craig, Strauss, Stephen J., and Tennent, Timothy C. *Encountering Theology of Mission: Biblical Foundations, Historical Developments, and Contemporary Issues.* Grand Rapids: Baker Academic, 2010.

Park, Andrew Sung. *The Wounded Heart of God: The Asian Concept of Han and the Christian Doctrine of Sin.* Nashville: Abington Press, 1993.

Park, Timothy K. *Mission History of Asian Churches.* Pasadena: William Carey Library, 2011.

Parratt, John. *A Reader in African Christian Theology.* London: SPCK, 1997.

Perriere, Benedictine Brac de la. "The Burmese Nat: Between Sovereignty and Autochthony." *Diogenes* 44/2, no. 174 (1996): 45.

Petri, Ludwig Adolph. *Mission and the Church: A Letter to a Friend.* Hanover: Hahn' schen Hofbuchhandlung, 1841. Translated by David Buchs, 8 February 2012.

Plantinga, Richard John. "Seeking the Boundaries: Gerardus van der Leeuw on the Study of Religion and the Nature of Theology." PhD diss., McMaster University, 1990.

Pool, Jeff B. *God's Wounds: Hermeneutic of the Christian Symbol of Divine Suffering.* Vol. 2. Cambridge: Luther worth Press, 2010. Accessed on 31 August 2021. doi:10.2307/j.cttlcgf8fn.

Price, Lynne, Juan Sepulveda, and Graeme Smith, eds. *Mission Matters.* Frankfurt: Peter Lang, 1997.

Ray, Niharranjan. *Theravada Buddhism in Burma*. 2nd ed. Bangkok: Orchid, 2006.
Reed, Lyman E. *Preparing Missionaries for Intercultural Communication*. Pasadena: William Carey Library, 1985.
Reimer, Johannes. *Missio Politica: The Mission of Church and Politics*. Carlisle: Langham Global Library, 2017.
Rheenen, Gailyn Van. *Communicating Christ in Animistic Contexts*. Pasadena: William Carey Library, 1991.
Robert, Dana L. *Christian Mission: How Christianity Became a World Religion*. Chichester: Wiley-Blackwell, 2009.
Rogers, Glenn. *A Basic Introduction to Missions and Missiology*. Bedford: Mission and Ministry Resources, 2003.
Sakhong, Lian Hmung. *In Defense of Identity: The Ethnic Nationalities' Struggle for Democracy, Human Rights and Federalism in Burma*. Bangkok: Orchid Press, 2010.
Saldana, Johnny. *The Coding Manual for Qualitative Researchers*. London: SAGE Publications, 2013.
Sangermano, Fr. Vinentious. *A Description of the Burmese Empire*. Translated by William Tandy. Rome: Joseph Salvucci & Son, 1833.
Schaeffer, Francis A. *How Should We Then Live?: The Rise and Decline of Western Thought and Culture*. New Jersey: Fleming H. Revell, 1976Schnabel, Eckhard J. *Paul the Missionary: Realities and Methods*. Downers Grove: IVP, 2008.
Schmidt-Leukel, Perry. *Buddhist Attitude to Other Religions*. Germany: EOS Edition of St. Ottilien, 2008.
Schober, Julian. *Modern Buddhist Conjunctures in Myanmar*. Honolulu: University of Hawaii Press, 2011.
Schulz, Gregory P. "Mission Communication," DMS923. Class lecture, Concordia Theological Seminary Fort Wayne, October 2019.
———. "The Word Became Flesh." Class lecture at Concordia Theological Seminary Fort Wayne, Winter 2019.
Schulz, Klaus Detlev. *Mission from the Cross: The Lutheran Theology of Mission*. St. Louis: Concordia Publishing, 2009.
Senior, Donald C. P., and Carroll C. P. Stuhlmueller. *The Biblical Foundations for Mission*. Maryknoll: Orbis Books, 1989.
Si, Oliver Byar Bowh. *God in Burma: Civil Society and Public Theology in Myanmar*. Milwaukee: Createspace, 2014.
Sire, James W. *The Universe Next Door*. Downers Grove: IVP, 2009.
Snyder, Howard A. *Global Good News: Mission in a New Context*. Nashville: Abington Press, 2001.
Spiro, Melford E. *Burmese Supernaturalism*. London: Routledge, 1996.
St. John, Graham. *Victor Turner and Contemporary Cultural Performance*. New York: Berghahn Books, 2008.

Stetzer, Ed, and Daniel Im. *Planting Missional Churches: Your Guide to Starting Churches That Multiply*. Nashville: B&H Academic, 2016.

Stevenson, H. N. C. *The Hill Peoples of Burma, Burma Pamphlets*. New York: Long Green, 1944.

Stott, John R. W. *Basic Christianity*. Downers Grove: IVP Books, 2008.

Sunquist, Scott W. *Understanding Christian Mission: Participation in Suffering and Glory*. Grand Rapids: Baker Academic, 2013.

Temple, Richard Carnac. *The Thirty-Seven Nat: A Phase of Spirit Worship Prevailing in Burma*. London: W. Griggs, 1906.

Terry, John Mark. *Missiology: An Introduction to the Foundations, History, and Strategies of World Missions*. Nashville: B&H Academic, 2016.

Than, U Kyaw. "The Christian Mission in Asia Today." *International Review of Mission* 47, no. 186 (April 1959): 154.

———. "What Mission Is." *Missiology: An International Review* 18, no. 4 (October 2011): 5.

Thang, Do Sian. "Toward a Theology of the New Year Water Festival, Thingyan, in Myanmar." *Thamar Alin* 4 (1999): 27.

The Holy Bible in Burmese. Translated from the Original Tongue. Gulfport: Bible Education and Missionary Service.

Trager, Helen G. *Burma through Aliens Eyes: Missionaries View of the Burmese in the Nineteenth Century*. New York: Frederick Praeger, 1966.

Tylor, Edward B. *Primitive Culture: Research into the Development of Mythology, Philosophy, Religion, Language, Art, and Custom*. Vol 1. London: Albmarble Street, 1891.

Vicedom, Georg F. *The Mission of God: An Introduction to a Theology of Mission*. St. Louis: Concordia Publishing, 1965.

Vine, W. E. *Expository Dictionary of Old & New Testament Worlds*. Nashville: Thomas Nelson Publishers, 1997.

Wa, Maung Shwe, and Genevieve Sowards. *Burmese Baptist Chronicle* Rangoon: Burma Baptist Convention Book I & II, 1962.

Walker, Graham B., Jr. "Building a Christian Zayat in the Shade of the Bo Tree." *American Baptist Quarterly* 32, no. 1 (Spring 2013): 14.

Walls, Andrew F. *The Missionary Movement in Christian History*. Maryknoll: Orbis Books, 1996.

Wiley, Don. "DMS975–Missiological Research Design." Class lecture and PowerPoints, Concordia Theological Seminary Fort Wayne, July 2019.

Wilson, Benjamin R. *The Saving Cross of the Suffering Christ*. Berlin: CPI Books, 2016.

Witherington, Ben, III. *New Testament History: A Narrative Account*. Grand Rapids: Baker Academic, 2001.

Wolcott, Harry F. *Ethnography: A Way of Seeing*. New York: Altamira Press, 2008.

Wright, Christopher J. H. *The Mission of God. Unlocking the Bible's Grand Narrative*. Downers Grove: IVP Academic, 2006.

Yong, Amos. *The Missiological Spirit: Christian Mission Theology in the Third Millennium Global Context*. Eugene: Cascade Books, 2014.

———. *Mission after Pentecost: The Witness of the Spirit from Genesis to Revelation*. Grand Rapids: Baker Academic, 2019.

Young, R. F. *Vain Debates: The Buddhist-Christian Controversies of Nineteenth Century Ceylon*. Vienna: The De Nobili Research Library, 1996.

Za Bik, Edmund. "Universal Salvation in the Context of Inter-faith Dialogue in Myanmar." *RAYS: MIT Journal of Theology* 11 (2008): 24.

Scripture Index

OLD TESTAMENT

Genesis
2:3 71
2:15 71
22:1–2 55

Exodus
14:14 14
20:8 71

1 Samuel
14:45 14

Isaiah
49:6 69

Jeremiah
1:4–5 69
14:22 48

Ezekiel
45:4 72

Zephaniah
3:17 109

NEW TESTAMENT

Matthew
1:21 65
16:18 45
28:19–20 .... 10, 102

Luke
1:31 65

John
1:1 43
1:14 43
14:6 65–66

Acts
2:23–24 51
7:1–38 71
11:19 58
11:22–23 58
14:8–18 46
14:11 41
14:15 .... 42, 48

15:20 47
17:23 46
19:24 46
19:27 47
19:27–28 46
19:28 46
20:24 57

Romans
1:1 .... 55, 69
1:15–16 69
1:18–32 48
3:10 37
3:23 37
6:23 58
8:11 68

1 Corinthians
1:23 54
8:1–11 46
12:2 48

15:12–14 68
15:50–58 51

2 Corinthians
5:17 70
5:19 118
5:20 119
11:13–14 101
12:9 57

Philippians
3:20–21 51

1 Thessalonians
1:9 48

Hebrews
4:16 57

2 Peter
3:18 57

Langham Literature, with its publishing work, is a ministry of Langham Partnership.

Langham Partnership is a global fellowship working in pursuit of the vision God entrusted to its founder John Stott –

> *to facilitate the growth of the church in maturity and Christ-likeness through raising the standards of biblical preaching and teaching.*

Our vision is to see churches in the Majority World equipped for mission and growing to maturity in Christ through the ministry of pastors and leaders who believe, teach and live by the word of God.

Our mission is to strengthen the ministry of the word of God through:
- nurturing national movements for biblical preaching
- fostering the creation and distribution of evangelical literature
- enhancing evangelical theological education

especially in countries where churches are under-resourced.

Our ministry

Langham Preaching partners with national leaders to nurture indigenous biblical preaching movements for pastors and lay preachers all around the world. With the support of a team of trainers from many countries, a multi-level programme of seminars provides practical training, and is followed by a programme for training local facilitators. Local preachers' groups and national and regional networks ensure continuity and ongoing development, seeking to build vigorous movements committed to Bible exposition.

Langham Literature provides Majority World preachers, scholars and seminary libraries with evangelical books and electronic resources through publishing and distribution, grants and discounts. The programme also fosters the creation of indigenous evangelical books in many languages, through writer's grants, strengthening local evangelical publishing houses, and investment in major regional literature projects, such as one volume Bible commentaries like the *Africa Bible Commentary* and the *South Asia Bible Commentary*.

Langham Scholars provides financial support for evangelical doctoral students from the Majority World so that, when they return home, they may train pastors and other Christian leaders with sound, biblical and theological teaching. This programme equips those who equip others. Langham Scholars also works in partnership with Majority World seminaries in strengthening evangelical theological education. A growing number of Langham Scholars study in high quality doctoral programmes in the Majority World itself. As well as teaching the next generation of pastors, graduated Langham Scholars exercise significant influence through their writing and leadership.

To learn more about Langham Partnership and the work we do visit **langham.org**

www.ingramcontent.com/pod-product-compliance
Lightning Source LLC
Chambersburg PA
CBHW070938180426
43192CB00039B/2318